# THE FATHER FACTOR
How Your Father's Legacy Impacts Your Career

"Every chapter and every paragraph presents powerful thoughts which every son, or father, for that matter, cannot run away from. Dr. Poulter discusses the 'undiscussable.' . . . He whittles away at the factors of success, failure, personal tribulation, and personal inferiority which accompany our daily ritual of going to work, caring for family, and trying to be better than our fathers and their expectations.

"With a focus on the personality 'carried' by our fathers, Dr. Poulter poignantly explains that our daily work life is impacted by that father-son relationship."

—Rory K. Zaks, president of sales for a national technology company

"Until reading *The Father Factor*, I had never connected my relationship with my father to the successes that I have experienced in my career. . . . Dr. Poulter details the impact of the father-child relationship and how, by understanding our experience, we can benefit and grow. As Dr. Poulter passionately emphasizes, relationships matter and fathers matter.

"*The Father Factor* is truly a gift of insight to the power of relationships."

—Tami Eldredge, investment banker

"Having never known my father or either of my grandfathers, it has been a considerable challenge to overcome that void in building my own successful entertainment litigation practice. The brilliance of Dr. Poulter's book is not only that he identifies the father factor as it impacts the careers of sons and daughters, but that he also establishes a formula for overcoming its often negative effects."

—Edwin F. McPherson, managing partner,
McPherson & Kalmansohn, LLP, Los Angeles, California

"First with *Father Your Son* and now with *The Father Factor*, Dr. Poulter illustrates the profound, lifelong effects our fathers and father figures have . . . both professional and personal. Coming to grips with those effects, especially the less positive ones, can confer equally profound benefits on our interpersonal relationships and help us understand why our own fathering, mentoring, and even managing styles have developed the way they have and what we can do to improve them."

—Gordon J. Louttit, business executive and lawyer

"In *The Father Factor*, Dr. Poulter provides a wonderfully readable and insightful roadmap to overcoming the workplace and career obstacles that our father's parenting style may have created for us."

—Eileen Gallo, PhD, coauthor of *Silver Spoon Kids* and *The Financially Intelligent Parent*

"The father factor is the missing element in the understanding of my company. This is the key I have been looking for. Dr. Poulter has addressed the invaluable long-term role fathers have in their children's career development."

—Bill Klem, president, W. S. Klem Contractor, Inc.

"Dr. Poulter offers an insightful look into a significant relationship that has helped shape who and how we are today. Very few of us can claim to have been raised by the ideal father. The resultant injuries, known or unknown, are impacting our lives as adults, constantly impeding our efforts to create satisfactory relationships in our personal and professional lives. The information that Dr. Poulter provides herein will help the reader attain the self-knowledge and understanding to remove these impediments."

—Barry Weichman, DDS

"I never would have thought to try to learn about employees' father factor in an effort to be a better manager. Dr. Poulter's book provides great insight not only for those trying to achieve career success, but also for manager/mentors trying to encourage others in their careers."

—Jean M. Clark, executive at an investment management firm

Stephan B. Poulter, PhD

# THE FATHER FACTOR
## How Your Father's Legacy Impacts Your Career

 Prometheus Books

97

Published 2006 by Prometheus Books

Inquiries should be addressed to
Prometheus Books
59 John Glenn Drive
Amherst, New York 14228–2197
VOICE: 716–691–0133, ext. 207
FAX: 716–564–2711
WWW.PROMETHEUSBOOKS.COM

10 09 08 07 06    5 4 3 2

Library of Congress Cataloging-in-Publication Data

Poulter, Stephan.
    The father factor : how your father's legacy impacts your career / by Stephan B. Poulter.
        p. cm.
    Includes bibliographical references and index.
    ISBN 1–59102–410–2 (pbk. : alk. paper)
    1. Psychology, Industrial. 2. Fatherhood—Psychological aspects. 3. Parental influences. 4. Socialization. 5. Self-evaluation. 6. Career development—Psychological aspects. I. Title.

HF5548.8.P634 2006
158.6—dc22

2006003367

Printed in the United States of America on acid-free paper

*To all the women and men who have struggled to find, understand, and use the father factor in positive ways that have changed them and the world they live in. This book is for people who know that fathers can simultaneously be a blessing and be a huge disappointment. That is why I dedicate this book to the adults who have overcome terrible father/child circumstances and have shared their stories with all of us. I am very touched by the personal, heart-felt stories that I have been privileged to learn about and share in this book. It is a tremendous opportunity on a personal level to write about this powerful topic: the father factor.*

To my daughter, Madison: *I know you don't understand the importance of fathers yet, but you have shown me the importance of daughters to their fathers. Without your wisdom, love, and insight, I would never be able to address father/daughter issues with the same degree of experience. You are my rose, queen, and diamond.*

To my son, Jonathan Brett: *At such a young age, you have always supported the role of fathers and my working with them. You are the son who never stops teaching me how to be a compassionate-mentor father. I am the luckiest man alive to be your dad.*

To my father, Peter Brett: *You showed me that the key of forgiveness was always in my hand and I never knew I held it. You are always in my heart, mind, and actions. Thanks, Dad.*

# OTHER BOOKS BY THE AUTHOR

*Mending the Broken Bough:*
*Restoring the Promise of the Mother-Daughter Relationship*

*Father Your Son:*
*How to Become the Father You Have Always Wanted to Be*

# AUTHOR'S NOTE

All the stories and voices contained in this book are derived in part from my clinical experience, research, law enforcement career, and ministry experience. However, the names, places, and other details contained in this book have been altered to protect the privacy and anonymity of individuals to whom they refer. Therefore, any similarity between the names and stories of the individuals and families described in this book and those individuals known to readers is inadvertent and purely coincidental.

The use of masculine pronouns and specific references to only fathers in this book are for the sole purpose of explaining the issues of fathers to their children. The apparent exclusion of feminine pronouns is for the purpose of writing, educating, and illustrating the subject matter only. The importance and relevance of mothers to this timeless topic is also covered.

# CONTENTS

# ACKNOWLEDGMENTS

M any thanks to all the people who have directly and indirectly contributed to the creation of this book. Special thanks to some key individuals whose support was invaluable during this process: Celia Rocks, for pushing me to formulate the father factor and put it in a written form; my editor, Linda Greenspan Regan, who gave me the opportunity to create this book; Julia Wolfe, for being my professional and spiritual mentor; Kye Hellmers, for writing the foreword and supporting the role of dads in their children's lives; and, last, my family, for lending their support.

I also want to thank my extended support network and father factor contributors: Kye and Kathleen Hellmers, William and Mary Klem, Dr. Barry Weichman, Ed MacPherson, Mike Costa, Dr. Eileen and Jon Gallo, Robert Brody, Marlene Clark, Dottie Dehart, Bruce Wexler, Mark Rubin, Rory Zaks, Winston Gooden, Mike Jones, Dave Lehr, Ed Vanderflet, Sandra Vasquez, Evan Carter, Drs. Chester and J. A. Semel, and Tamika Eldredge. Without these types of people in my life (past and present) and career, I could never have ventured out of my professional box and addressed such a powerful, life-changing subject as this one. This book could not have been what it is without the effort and dedication of all involved. I thank all of you.

# FOREWORD

Remember the thrills you experienced when your dad taught you how to ride a bike? Is it possible you also received, at the very same time, important information you would use years later to help shape your interpersonal relationships—in the workplace? According to Dr. Stephan B. Poulter, the answer is an emphatic yes!

In this, his latest book, Dr. Poulter asks us to dive headfirst into the personal relationship that we each had with our father since infancy and to learn to understand its impact on our careers. You will find that he pulls no punches as he asks us to look, in stark, honest terms, at the "type" of person our father was and that we realize and accept how this "type" determined how we interact with others.

Dr. Poulter's overriding message is clear: "Fathers matter." They do, whether the relationship was good, bad, or otherwise. They matter very much. And that means they affect us very much.

*The Father Factor* introduces us to five primary fathering "styles," ranging from the most desirable, the "compassionate-mentor," to the least, the "abusive" and the "time-bomb" fathers. Can a father exhibit multiple style traits? Sure. Frankly, it would be difficult to imagine someone who didn't. But each father has a clear predisposition toward one primary style. And, remarkably, this remains, as Dr. Poulter says, "overarching, consistent, and ongoing."

This, to me, is the crux of *The Father Factor*. We are, each and every one of us, awash with behaviors derived from our fathers' style. They developed from shared experiences—from the first hug to a complete loss or absence of contact. And, whether or not we like it, these experiences are now part of us. Not hardwired as, for example, our height or the color of our skin, but pretty darn close—it's more like some software program installed a long, long time ago that undergoes constant updating. Little wonder this relationship has such consequence.

Today, it seems that more and more people are questioning their careers in new and, interestingly, largely nonfinancial terms—in more abstract and human terms, in terms where success seems driven more by values and less by money. Not so sure? Well, have you ever heard anyone say, "I don't like my boss, and I think my coworkers are all a bunch of idiots, but I'm paid well, so I really love my job"? Of course not. You might very well love the field you're in or the type of work you do, maybe even the firm itself. And let's hope you are satisfied financially. But if you do not have positive, well-constructed relationships extending in every direction, providing you with proper feedback and recognition, you cannot possibly *love* your job. You may also be inadvertently positioning yourself to fail.

More than ever before, people increasingly find themselves working in supercharged environments where they have to constantly adjust to events over which they have no real control—things like longer hours, fewer vacation days, shrinking benefits, and increased workloads. How these issues are dealt with (and they *are* dealt with) depends, in no small measure, on workplace relationships.

We also know there are innumerable other events arising daily in the workplace that must similarly be managed. Transitory in nature, unpredictable, and, often, overlapping (or nearly so), these are, perhaps, even more important because how we react serves as mortar for the very building blocks we use in constructing and maintaining our interpersonal relationships. Consider: it's early in the workday, and you've just left your boss's office, where you received a compliment for a job well done ("I'm a success!"), when Joan, your coworker, confronts you angrily because you failed to meet a deadline ("I'm a failure"). Wow! You have just arrived at the intersection of opposite and conflicting assessments of your work. You will react. On top of this, you will also react to the *many* other successes, failures, irritations, joys, and disappointments you are sure to encounter throughout the rest of the day—probably before lunch.

*The Father Factor* offers guidance on how to assimilate and respond to these issues in a way that does not lead to second-guessing, self-recrimination, or failure but rather in a manner designed to enhance the building and maintenance of proper relationships—ultimately promoting positive career development and job satisfaction.

This, then, is the fundamental reason that I believe *The Father Factor* is so important: it opens the door to the most revealing and important self-discovery possible—that which concerns how and why we interact with others as we do and guides us toward effecting positive change.

What I enjoyed most about *The Father Factor* was the chance to relive so many wonderful memories of my dad as they came rushing back. A bit of background: I'm the oldest of three children; my sister and I were adopted; my brother, the youngest, was my parents' biological child. Dad died in 1983 and Mom, the next year. I remember Dad in various ways: as a pretty tough guy who came out of one the poor sections of Brooklyn, New York; as a World War II veteran who drove a tank across Europe; as a high school graduate; as a teamster; as a man called "Dutch" (during less sensitive times when such nicknames were considered endearing). He was one whose gentleness was hidden behind a gruff exterior, who always had time, who put his family first, and whose wife and children were never hungry, cold, or unprotected. He was also flawed, and I know his flaws have had an effect on my childhood and my personal and business lives—but so have his good points. I love and miss him very much.

Simply put, Dr. Poulter is one of the most qualified people I know in this area of study. He is a recognized authority on parent/child relationships whose education, training, experience, and temperament make him well suited to offer this expert helping hand. And, perhaps most important, he is a loving and devoted father (in the style of the compassionate-mentor) to Jonathan and Madison, his children. He is also my friend.

I believe one of our greatest gifts is our ability to understand. Given this, *The Father Factor* holds out the promise of taking us further along the path to understanding ourselves and others than we could otherwise manage on our own. Thanks, Stephan.

And thanks, too, Dad.

Kye Hellmers, a father and a son
October 2005

Section I

# THE BASICS OF THE FATHER FACTOR

# Chapter 1

## FATHERS MATTER
### The Impact on What You Do and How You Do It

It wasn't until after my third personnel conflict with a male supervisor within a six-month period that I noticed a troubling pattern. It was only then [I had] the idea that my relationship with my father might have something to do with my career problems.

—Linda, age twenty-nine

I have always wanted and sought my father's approval. I rarely received his support and approval. I still look for it at times with colleagues and clients. It is a vicious cycle: I want my father's support, and I know it will never happen the way I want it to—he isn't that kind of man.

—Mike, age thirty-seven

Some people are very skeptical about the impact their fathers have had on their careers, especially if they've chosen jobs that are different from their dads'. "I'm a lawyer, and my father was an electrician, so obviously he hasn't had any influence" is a typical response to being asked whether one's father had any effect on one's career choice.

The father factor exerts its influence in many different ways, not just whether you followed in dad's professional footsteps. It can create your most significant weakness on the job as well as your most significant strength. It can determine your level of job satisfaction. And it applies to women as well as to men, to the middle-aged as well as to young people. It is a timeless influence that must be properly understood if you're going to maximize your individual potential and ability in your career and life. *The foundation for your career direction, the father factor directs your career selection and development, both consciously and unconsciously; your ability to excel; and your ability to develop meaningful professional relationships. Your father's particular parenting style is the template that forms the father factor in your career.*

If you're still wondering about its existence, try an experiment. Think about a conflict with a boss or a subordinate that occurred relatively recently. Perhaps your boss called you into his office to complain about your performance on a recent project. Perhaps you had to put a subordinate on probation. Whatever the episode involved, summarize it in a paragraph, focusing on your words and feelings at that moment. For instance:

> I told Joan that I could not tolerate her talking rudely to our major customer again. I explained that I realized this customer could be a pain but that her behavior was inexcusable. For the next fifteen minutes or so, I talked while she listened; I essentially gave her a refresher course on how to treat our clients, Customer Service 101. I said, "I know you think the customer is a jerk, but you should be mature enough not to lash out at him the way you did." As I was talking to her, I felt a bit guilty because Joan is a good person and solid employee, and the customer was truly a jerk.

After writing your paragraph, answer the following questions:

1. Did what you say in the encounter remind you in any way of how your father spoke to you when you were a child?
2. Is there anything that you said that was either the exact opposite of or identical to the tone and substance of your father's conversations with you?
3. Were your feelings in this encounter similar to or the exact opposite of those you experienced when you had a conflict with your dad as a child?

The odds are that, even without going through this formal exercise, you've experienced situations in which your words or feelings at work reminded you of an encounter with your father. People commonly report talking to a subordinate exactly how their fathers talked to them, even to the point of using the same expressions. They also frequently recall relating to a boss in the same way that they related to their father. In other instances, though, the impact of a father on an adult child's work behaviors is more subtle than many would expect. This effect is the theme of this entire book and will be looked at from many different perspectives and under numerous circumstances.

The key, however, is recognizing that there is an impact. The father factor is a negative in your career only if it goes unrecognized and undiscovered. When you're aware of it and learn to manage it, this factor becomes a positive force. Therefore, let's look at some issues that should raise your awareness of the profound impact your father has on your life and your career.

## AN IMPACT THAT TRANSCENDS DEATH, GENDER, AND INTIMACY

One obstacle to appreciating the profound effect of the father factor is rationalizing it away. For example:

- My father has been dead for fifteen years; how could he still have an impact on my career?
- I'm a woman, so it makes more sense that my mother rather than my father has affected my career choices and job performance.
- I was never particularly close with my father, so I don't think he has much of an impact.
- My father was a nonprofessional and worked at the same job for forty-two years until his retirement. I am already a professional, have had two career changes, and have never worked longer than four years at any one company.
- I never respected my father's work ethic or his work history. I am completely different.

Let's look at why each of these rationalizations are specious.

If your father has died, that doesn't mean that the feelings from that relationship are dead. Many of the most important relationships we will have in our lifetimes are timeless. We carry the impact of these relationships in our minds and hearts. When women and men of all ages talk to me about the death of their fathers, even the people who maintain that they didn't have a close relationship with their dads say that they were surprised by how much they were affected. People routinely use terms such as *devastating* and *over-*

*whelming loss* to describe their reactions. It is not unusual for daughters and sons, then, to suffer from depression and hopelessness and/or to begin to question life's meaning. It is also common for adult children to question and ponder their careers after their fathers' death. Suddenly, a job that they liked may appear trivial and meaningless.

Years later, this death still has tremendous power and influence. When some consider leaving a job long after their fathers have passed away, a number of them note that they can hear their fathers' voices in their head, "I didn't raise any child of mine to be a quitter," and they heed that voice. When others decide to make a significant career change, they often explain it by saying, "I didn't want to end up dying like my dad and never having had a chance to do what I really wanted to do." Therefore, don't underestimate the impact of your father on your career. If your father is dead, recall the enormity of your feelings about him at the time of his death. If he's alive, talk to trusted colleagues or friends whose dads have passed away and ask them whether their career decisions have been affected by the memory of their fathers.

Many women—in fact, some men—believe that their mothers had more influence than their fathers did over the adult professional they became. No one would argue the commonsense logic that mothers are invaluable to their children's development. In fact, in the world of stay-at-home moms and often emotionally or physically absent dads in which many of us grew up, mothers had the greatest impact on our lives simply because they were there the majority of the time. Women certainly are role models for their daughters, and it would be absurd to suggest that fathers are models for their daughters in the same way. And because of a distant relationship between many fathers and daughters, their dads are discounted in terms of importance and long-term career influence.

Despite all this, however, most of you from the baby boom generation were probably were raised with a man as the primary breadwinner in your family. In the prototypical nuclear family or some combination of it, Dad wore a suit, work clothes, or a uniform and went to work every day, while Mom was a homemaker. Even if your mother worked, she was probably viewed—overtly or more subtly—as second in importance from a work and financial perspective.

Typically, men made more money; they didn't take time off to have children or to raise them; and they had "real" jobs (doctor, lawyer, businessman) as opposed to women, who primarily were in the helping professions (teacher, nurse, social worker). It is extremely important to note that being a teacher, nurse, or social worker is by no means less demanding or important than the traditional male professions. There was—and still is, at times—a cultural bias against women that has been in place for many years. Though things have changed quite a bit in recent years, typically men still are paid more than women even in careers such as law, medicine, engineering, and business (especially at the top corporate levels); men are still less likely than women to stay at home and raise the children. Women are still considered the primary parents for their children regardless of their career status. Those women raised in a traditional home need to understand their mothers' legacy in the home and also their fathers' legacy in the business world, for these daughters have a double-edged sword approach to their career. One side is their fathers' role and work ethic. The other is their mothers' approach and view of the working woman. It is critical for all daughters to understand each parent's beliefs about the home and workplace. It may be very difficult for a daughter to reconcile her dad's professional accomplishments against her own professional competence and her mother's views of what women should be doing.

For these reasons, along with thousands of years of human history, fathers have generally had a more significant impact on a child's career choices and work habits than mothers have had. The workplace has always been a masculine model and arena for men, and men have been solely defined by their work and the success within it. Most men still view a failed career opportunity as a personal failure, and many women feel the same way about men who don't succeed in their jobs. The home, on the other hand, has been a feminine model for women. Women have been defined by how well they cared for their children and tended to home duties. Right, wrong, or otherwise, these cultural beliefs are very strong and have been in place for thousands of years. Fathers have always been expected to work the land or, since the Industrial Revolution, work away from the home and support all their family's material and financial needs and wants. In family law court, however, the majority of child custody cases are settled in favor of the mother having both the legal and physical custody of the children. The reason is that, regardless of the father's emotional and mental fitness, women are viewed as better primary parents. More and more men and women are challenging these types of cultural stereotypes, but there is considerable wisdom for a daughter and son to gain from understanding the effect of their father's work ethic in relation to their beliefs about their own professional lives.

In terms of the third objection—that because a child wasn't close to a father, the father probably didn't have much of an impact—the opposite is usually true. We live in a society where fathers are often emotionally absent at home; they cede much of the parenting responsibility to moms. Children possess a natural psychological and emotional need for both parents to be present, and, when one isn't, a negative effect can result. When dads are absent, the effect usually is most keenly felt in areas such as a work ethic, ambition, and relating to authority figures. Fathers matter to their children, and all children naturally crave their fathers' involvement in their lives.

Absence, of course, isn't the only issue that causes career problems for a child. A father-child relationship that is problematic, strained, or filled with anger and disappointment may have a profound effect on everything from career choices to relationships with colleagues. As negative as this might seem, there's a positive flip side to it. The relationship with your father (or stepfather or any male father figure) can provide you with a wealth of information and insight—and that goes even for a bad relationship! You can use this information and insight to get back on track or to move your performance to the next level. Understanding your father's legacy in terms of relationships, work, and finances can be a powerful resource and springboard for your career.

Believing that your father's career has no relevance to your own is often myopic and dangerous. Let's say, for instance, that your father started working for General Electric right after the war and stayed with the company for forty-eight years in a nonmanagement capacity until his retirement. You have gone to college, have an advanced degree, have worked in several management positions, and have been laid off twice as a result of corporate mergers. It appears on the surface that your and your father's career lives have nothing in common. Consider, for a minute, your father's motivation, certain career choices, work stability/endurance, and relationship style. These nonverbal daily behaviors contributed to the very fabric and foundation of your own father factor. Even if you're a woman, you have your own father factor, which is your style of behaving, professionally and otherwise, which was influenced by your father. You observed your father in his career and watched him survive in the same place for forty-eight years. Your father's work behaviors contributed valuable pointers on how to conduct yourself in your career. There are considerable nuggets of information and wisdom to be found in how your father survived in the workplace, managed difficult supervisors, and remained in the same job for so many years. Don't dismiss his career life because it appears so different from yours. The same tools can be useful for you to survive in your career as they were for your father.

Finally, your father may not have been a career role model or the type of person you care to emulate. The slippery slope of anger, resentment, and rage in this relationship is one that many daughters and sons, regardless of age, fall into, desperately trying to become the professional that their father never was. This career approach is a reaction to the family trauma that you experienced growing up. There is an edge of aggressiveness and "cold-heartedness" to professionals who have never resolved or come to terms with who and what their father was. The driving force in this son's or daughter's career is the complete rejection of who and what their father was as a parent, working adult, and partner to his or her mother.

The career legacy is overcoming the disappointment and disillusionment of men. Trust of authority figures is a difficult thing for professionals who have had this type of father-child relationship.

## HOW THE FATHER FACTOR WORKS: THE MANY SOURCES OF ITS POWER

The father factor can work *for* you or *against* you; it all depends on whether you understand and appreciate it or ignore it. Let us assume you prefer the former. The key to understanding and appreciating depends on looking at the father-child relationship from the following perspectives.

1. *The four different types of attachment (your emotional bond with your father).* The four types—intermittent, avoidant, depressed, and secure—provide clues on how you connect emotionally in personal and professional relationships. (They are described in detail in chapter 2). It shouldn't be surprising that people who formed a secure attachment with their dads when they were young usually enjoy strong, beneficial work and intimate relationships. A secure attachment means that a child and his father bonded early in the relationship and maintained that bond, giving the child a strong sense of security and a feeling of being loved. This attachment process pro-

vided a basis for all future relationships, allowing the adult-child to be open, communicative, and trusting of other people. Of course, not all attachments are equally positive. By understanding this bond, even under the worst of circumstances, you can still develop secure, strong emotional bonds with people.

2. *Your father's rule book: your father's and grandfather's spoken and unspoken rules about work, relationships, ethics, and money matters.* Hard work, ambition, and achievement are learned behaviors in families. The odds are that if you're highly successful, so, too, was your father and his father before him. While there are many exceptions to this rule, it generally holds that sons and daughters follow in the footsteps of their fathers and their grandfathers concerning work. Even more predictable are the rules of the ways of relating, which are *all* based on your internal rule book. This comprises powerful spoken and unspoken rules, which guide your behavior, thoughts, and beliefs. Once you are aware of your father's rule book, you have to update, rewrite, and make it all yours. Most adults live by their book but seldom consider changing the outdated, nonproductive behaviors in it. Your father handed this rule book to you, but it must be reread, rewritten, and re-evaluated for your career to move forward.

3. *Fathering style (daily interactions, behaviors, and communication with your father).* The five basic styles of fathering are the superachiever, the time bomb, the passive/negligent father, the absent father, and the compassionate-mentor (which are discussed in detail in chapters 3–8). These have a tremendous effect on your own work style, relationship style, and the rules by which you live. Whether you are a harsh and demanding boss or a pushover depends, to a significant extent, on your father's parenting style. How your father interacted with you is a critical piece of personal information that helped shape your current career choices, professional relationships, and career potential. Understanding fathering styles provides the foundation for insight into the father factor and thus into your career and personal life.

## Sam's Story

To give you a sense how these three areas of daily interaction, behavior, and communication with your father influence jobs and careers, let's take a look at the case of Sam, a thirty-eight-year-old associate with a small Cleveland law firm. Sam's dad, Teddy, was a salesman who was frequently on the road. Sam remembers weeks going by without seeing or even hearing from his dad, who drove throughout the Midwest selling machinery parts to factories. Even when Teddy was around the house, though, he wasn't particularly involved with Sam's life except when it came to sports. An avid sports fan and former minor league pitcher, Teddy paid attention to Sam only when he had a little league game—he would go to all the games, or, if he was on the road, he would call Sam after the game and ask how it went.

Though Teddy was often away because of work, he didn't work especially hard, or so it seemed to Sam. In fact, he was fired from the machinery-parts company because the company felt he wasn't "pulling his weight"— Sam remembered hearing the phrase during an argument his parents had. Over the next ten years or so, Teddy moved from one sales job to the next, never making much money or expressing much satisfaction with his work; his most common comment when he left a company or lost a position was, "It's just a job."

Sam, a good student, knew from the time he was in high school that he wanted to become a lawyer. He was extremely logical and an excellent debater—he won awards when he was on the high school debate team—and eventually attended one of the country's top law schools and made *Law Review* (a ranking of the top law students in the country). After graduating, he was offered a high-paying job with one of Cleveland's large corporate law firms. Shortly thereafter, he married and had two children.

Unfortunately, Sam's career didn't take off as it seemed like it might have. From the very start, he told his wife that he felt like a "round peg in a square hole" at the law firm. He hated the demeaning way that partners treated associates, and, once he had children, he adamantly refused to travel more than once a month on firm business, even though all the other associates traveled at least twice as much as Sam. On more than one occasion, Sam had what he termed "personality clashes" with partners, generally over issues that had nothing to do with the work and everything to do with their "attitudes." When Sam was passed over for partner, he resigned, telling his wife that he wanted to work for a smaller firm where the culture was more civilized and the hours more reasonable. Sam, though, had issues at every small firm he worked for. At one firm, his boss was lazy and incompetent. At another, the work wasn't sufficiently challenging. Though he didn't change firms as frequently as his father changed employers, he worked for five different firms in twelve years, and he didn't make partner at any of them.

How did Teddy impact Sam's career path, performance, and job satisfaction? First, Teddy was an intermittent or avoidant father emotionally. Teddy's fathering style was primarily absent, even though they lived together. At best, Teddy was a passive father toward Sam. Consequently, Sam grew up without ever establishing a secure emotional attachment with his dad. In turn, he tended to be wary of most people, especially bosses. He never fully trusted them or believed what they told him—the result of an absent father. Sam tended to leave law firms prematurely, perhaps because he unconsciously didn't want to be dismissed, as his father seemed to dismiss him. Second, Teddy was never a particularly positive role model in his treatment of money or ambition; he never made a lot of money or seemed to care much about achievement. While Sam outwardly wanted to do well and avoid his father's career path—he had chosen law because he not only had the talent for it but also figured he could make more money and travel less than in other jobs—he seemed to always sabotage himself professionally.

Just about every employer recognized Sam's talent, but it was his attitude that prevented him from rising above marginal status. Sam always seemed to be complaining about something, and his attitude negatively affected his relationships with clients. On more than one occasion, clients mentioned to Sam's colleagues or bosses that he seemed "disinterested" or at least not fully engaged. This may well have been a result of Teddy's avoidant/absent style of fathering. Except for when Sam played baseball, Teddy had rarely showed much emotion or interest in his son. Although Sam was much more emotionally aware and involved with his kids than Teddy was, he was different at work, putting a barrier between himself and others. He had an excellent legal mind and did solid work, but he didn't connect with clients or colleagues. Sam was more like his father at work than he could ever have imagined, wanted, or guessed.

In thinking about Sam's problems, you should be aware that he was bewildered and deeply frustrated by his inability to develop to the level expected, after having been a law school star. It was only after twelve years of career misfires and with the benefit of hindsight, reflection, and psychotherapy that Sam began to see how his father factor had affected him. Not surprisingly, Sam finally made partner at a midsized law firm when he became aware of how Teddy was still subtly influencing his job choices and attitude. Through his growing awareness, Sam took control of his father factor and made it into a positive influence. Sam was very careful not to blame his father or their strained relationship for his career frustration.

## REALITIES AND MISPERCEPTIONS OF FATHERS

People experience difficulty overcoming negative career legacies in large part because they don't see how the events that took place years ago at home could possibly affect their current careers. This is a very common career oversight. Sam, for instance, labored under a number of misconceptions, not only about his father and his impact on his career but about larger father-child issues. Such misperceptions cause us to minimize or dismiss things our fathers said and did when we were growing up. Many of us convince ourselves that we exist only in the here and now and that what's past remains in the past. Ironically, this attitude gives those past events more power than they ordinarily would have. When we pretend that a domineering, demeaning, demanding, or abusive father could have no effect on us today, we may unconsciously steer clear of or leave any job where the boss is "tough or critical," missing some great career opportunities and never understanding why.

When you become aware of the realities versus the misperceptions, however, you are much more likely to recognize—and do something constructive about—how your unconscious drives affect your career decisions. This awareness will also help you take advantage of all the ideas and tools that we will be discussing. By understanding your father factor, you will began to increase your level of personal and professional satisfaction, and then maximize your career potential.

The following true/false statements address some of the more common misperceptions of fathers and their impact on a daughter or son. Mark a T or an F next to each statement, then look at the answer key to determine how well you did. It is not important that you pass this quiz with flying colors. What is important is that you start to see the father-child relationship themes—ones that will increase your awareness of how your father's words and deeds have shaped your career choices and job performance.

1. Fathers and mothers serve the same role in raising their children.
2. Sons and daughters learn assertiveness and confidence from their

fathers and emotional intelligence from their mothers. (Emotional intelligence is the ability to have empathy, understanding, and insight into your interactions and impact on others.)

3. Biological fathers have no more influence on their sons than stepfathers or other nonbiological father figures.
4. Women and men can overcome a fatherless past and develop a positive father factor model.
5. Fathers affect their sons and daughters for their entire lives.
6. It is impossible for women and men to learn anything of value from fathers they hate(d).
7. Not all girls and boys crave or need a positive relationship with their dads.
8. Once men and women reach a certain age, they don't want their father's approval.
9. The emotional and mental wounds people suffered as kids prevent them from being successful in their careers.
10. Even when they're quite young, children pay close attention to their fathers' attitudes and behavior about work and the value of money.
11. Verbal abuse by your father is much less harmful than physical abuse.
12. While people who seem to have come to terms with a negative father-child relationship present calm façades in the workplace, they in fact are usually pressure cookers beneath the surface.

## Answers

1. False. Fathers serve as role models for their sons and daughters relative to how they approach work, use problem-solving abilities, and pursue career objectives. Mothers also serve as role models, but primarily for values and relationship issues and as a female balance to the father's influence. Each parent serves an invaluable but distinct role in a child's development. It is important to begin to understand your father's contribution to your career development. Your father plays a role today in your career.
2. False. The three primary emotions are love, fear, and anger, and the more a father is able to communicate these emotions to his kids in healthy, productive ways, the more likely they will develop emo-

tional intelligence in the workplace as adults. Personality conflicts between work colleagues can be traced back to our inability to express and understand these three primary emotions.

3. True. Fathering is not limited to biology. The term *stepfather* is a legal term, but in a relational context, the prefix *step* has little bearing on a man's true effectiveness as a father. Your career choices and work persona can be influenced by a man who was not your biological father but who played a significant role in your upbringing. It's also possible that more than one person—a biological father and a stepfather—can have a huge impact on your work choices and attitudes.

4. True. Not having a father or having a horrible relationship with him does not sentence you to repeat the past or continue the negative legacy. You can make the necessary changes to excel in your career, as well as in your personal life and relationships. Your ability to understand rather than blame your father is one of the keys to success, and it's the basis for the father factor model. While anger and hatred are strong short-term motivators, these two emotions can't sustain your career or meet all the demands necessary to develop professionally and personally.

5. True. Even after your father dies, he will still affect your professional relationships and career development. No matter what boys or girls say to their fathers in a fit of anger—for example, "I'll never be like you"—or how much they try to distance themselves as adults, their dads still cast a long shadow. Typically, people undervalue their fathers' impact on their lives until their parents' death. Even then, many men and women don't see how a father's influence extends past personal traits into the professional world. The values you carry concerning work were formed many years ago in the context and backdrop of your father-daughter or father-son relationship.

6. False. All daughters and sons learned an enormous number of things from their father. It is quite possible to move emotionally beyond your anger and hatred of your father. Analyzing the father-child relationship can yield valuable insights that will help make you a better manager, supervisor, and parent. These insights can help you make the necessary adjustments in your professional relationships and move you to your next career level.

7. False. At times, some young boys seem as if they do not need their

fathers, especially in the wake of a bitter divorce or a sudden remarriage. Some girls also appear to be so independent or so close to their mothers that they foster the illusion that a relationship with their father is of no consequence. In reality, every son and daughter seeks and needs a relationship with his or her father. The craving for an emotional fatherly bond must be emotionally acknowledged. Denying this natural impulse creates a void, one that plays itself out in work situations. People who deny this may also be in denial about the need to build strong relationships with customers, subordinates, and others.

8. False. *Regardless of age, we all desire our father's approval.* Approval is part of our psychological wiring and a natural occurring father-child dynamic. Unfortunately, you, like many kids, may never have received that approval growing up—or received it rarely. Giving your own self-approval, self-acceptance, and self-love is the solution, but many people choose instead to seek these qualities from others in the workplace. Many times, they look to a boss for fatherly approval, which, as we'll see in later chapters, creates all types of career and personal problems. Issues that result from missing/absent fathers will never be adequately resolved in the workplace.

9. False. Growing up with a conflicted, abusive father is not a reason to repeat the sins of the past or continue to punish yourself through your career choices. You don't have to run from bosses who offer constructive criticism or run to bosses who are weak and ineffectual, for instance. Nor do you have to become abusive to your subordinates in response to that childhood abuse. You control your career choices through insight about how you were raised and the style of fathering that shaped your childhood.

10. True. Sons and daughters watch their fathers like hawks when it comes to things involving money and work. Many children developed the skill of observing these work-related behaviors from a distance, without being noticed. Some people contend that they never really paid much attention to these issues while growing up. But usually they're just blocking out what may have been unpleasant experiences: Dad screaming at Mom for spending his hard-earned money or Dad complaining about how his boss has dumped too

many projects on him and he's thinking of quitting. Your approach to money and a work ethic come directly from observing your father's attitudes, actions, and beliefs in these two areas.

11. False. As horrific as physical abuse is, verbal abuse is equally destructive from a career standpoint. Cruel words and constant, negative badgering diminish a child's sense of self and lead to problems with authority and trust. Bosses who demean and belittle employees often come from homes where their fathers were verbally abusive; these people need to diminish others in order to build themselves up. (It is a constant cycle of abuse.) In addition, verbal abuse is invisible. Unlike most physically abused children, the verbally abused girl grows up believing she had a normal childhood. This lack of awareness makes her vulnerable to the effects of this abuse in the workplace and in intimate relationships, too. She often doesn't seek professional help for the damage done to her self-esteem and never acknowledges or articulates how awful she feels about her father's behavior—both past and present. Given the lack of overt physical evidence (broken arms, black-and-blue bruises, swollen faces), she tends to minimize the long-term damage that verbal abuse causes. Consequently, she carries the emotional damage and pain into both her personal and professional lives.

12. True. People in management positions often have perfected the art of appearing outwardly calm under pressure, while inside the pressure builds. These symptoms can cause sleepless nights, ulcers, and anxiety as well as physical problems that negatively affect their decision-making abilities or even cause them to quit. An emotionally supportive, caring father provides a child with the inner resources necessary to cope with all types of stress, including job-related pressures. He helps his child gain the self-esteem and coping skills that serve him well in school, work situations, and adult relationships. Some of these children may respond to stress with anger, depression, or anxiety, but inside they're capable of managing the stress and continuing to function effectively.

## PUTTING IT TOGETHER:
## CONNECTING THE FATHER'S BEHAVIOR WITH THE
## ADULT CHILD'S WORK ATTITUDES AND ACTIONS

Depending on attachment type, fathering style, and his rule book, a father can affect his children's career decisions and job behaviors in myriad ways. The effects, however, are far from uniform or clear to sons and daughters. Even if you have two dads (divorce from or remarriage to your mother) with the same attachment types, fathering styles can impact children in different ways—for example, a stepfather who is more emotional in his active fathering style than the biological father. Genetics and work environment (type of employer, culture, boss, etc.) also play significant roles. Still, we can make some clear connections between the way a father raised his children and the strengths and weaknesses they exhibit as professionals.

To help you see these connections, I've put together the following "quiz." You'll find a scenario describing a child, his father's methods of raising him, and then three possible outcomes for the child, when he or she becomes a working adult. See if you can make the connection between the child, the method of raising a child, and the likely outcome.

1. Andrew, a top corporate executive who worked extremely hard and did very well at his job, gave his daughter, Allison, nearly everything that she asked for while she was growing up. He did so in part because he had to travel a great deal for his job and often felt guilty for not being around much. Therefore, whenever he returned from a business trip, he had a present for Allison. In fact, he gave her a brand new BMW sports car for her sixteenth birthday, in addition to private tennis and golf lessons and trips to Europe during summer vacations with her college friends. He doted on Allison and rarely, if ever, raised his voice to her, even when she would get in trouble—staying out past curfew, getting speeding or reckless-driving tickets, drinking and driving. Andrew was certain that Allison was a great kid with strong values and that the best thing he could do as a parent was to trust her. He didn't demand or set any emotional or behavioral limits for Allison. Andrew wanted to be Allison's friend, first and foremost.

   A.  Allison became a successful corporate executive just like her father. She chose to follow in his footsteps because he treated her with such generosity and communicated his happiness with his career and the success that it brought him. She, too, was a high-powered executive who traveled a great deal, worked long hours, and was satisfied by the rewards of a top position and high salary.

B. Allison rejected the corporate world and materialism in general, rebelling in postadolescent fashion. She became an elementary school teacher at an inner-city school.

C. Allison bounced from job to job and career to career, never sticking with anything long enough to achieve any real measure of success or security. Though she would start a new career or job with enthusiasm, she quickly tired of it and became anxious to move on to something else. Allison had chronic financial problems and a poor credit rating. She needed her father to bail her out with large yearly donations.

Correct answer: C. An absent, overindulgent father can produce a child who finds that no boss or organization treats her as well as her dad did. She never receives enough praise, and her salary is never sufficient. She also finds that the work is never as easy or as much fun as she thought it would be. A result: she is constantly searching for the ideal job or career, a search that is futile. This type of father breeds a dependent daughter or son as a result of his passive/absent, overindulgent, guilt-driven style of fathering.

2. Michael, a self-employed plumber, was highly critical of and short-tempered with his son, Alex. In little league, Michael was the type of dad who yelled at Alex from the stands when he committed an error, and Michael constantly offered his son "tips" about how to play the game. When Alex would bring home his report card, Michael would never be satisfied, no matter how many A's Alex received. Michael exploded at his son for minor violations of the family rules, chewing him out in front of his friends and other family members. Michael did these things in part because this was how he himself was raised; his own father had made it clear that boys needed tough dads, or they were likely to get into terrible trouble.

A. Alex started his own small business that he operated out of his own home. He was able to make a living, but he passed on many opportunities to expand the business and make a much better living because, as he told others, he didn't want to take unnecessary risks. Alex was very unsure of himself and wasn't willing to extend himself.

B. Alex became a tyrannical boss, the type of old-fashioned command-and-control leader who barked orders and let people know if he was unhappy with their performance.

C. Alex became a stockbroker who relished in taking gambles and making them pay off. As a successful stockbroker, he showed the world (and his father) that he didn't deserve to be criticized.

Correct answer: A. As a result of Alex's upbringing, he was terrified of taking risks and being criticized for them should they fail. A small, safe, home-based business ensured that he wouldn't have many people angry at him or telling him what he was doing wrong. Alex couldn't tolerate having people upset with him and was very vigilant in keeping the peace with all the people in his life. Being self-employed also helped avoid the issue of dealing with any type of authority figure.

3. Carl, a dentist, made certain decisions early on to ensure that he could spend a lot of time with his son, Louis. He located his office relatively near his home, and he hired two associate dentists as soon as it was financially feasible, so he could then attend all of Louis's recitals and concerts. (Louis played the piano.) Not only did he spend time with Louis, but he was an emotionally present father. He wasn't afraid of expressing his emotions in front of his son; he didn't hide his tears when something sad occurred, and he also was willing to let Louis know if he was disappointed in him. Carl wasn't perfect—he tended to do things for Louis that Louis should have done himself—but he was a consistently compassionate and present.

A. Louis never could rise above mediocrity in his career, in part because his father gave him too much help and support and prevented him from being a self-starter; Louis, too, tried to be a dentist but lacked the initiative necessary to market and run his office effectively. Louis needed his father's emotional support so he could function in his career. Without it, he was ineffective.

B. Louis chose a completely different occupation from his father—he became the general manager of a major symphony orchestra—and loved what he did. He chose a field with relatively few positions, but he was confident in his ability to succeed at something he enjoyed and of which he was knowledgeable. A dynamic, creative executive, Louis helped his symphony orchestra stay in the black when most orchestras were losing money.

C. Louis became a studio musician and did fairly well, though he always wanted to play at a higher level. Carl was so supportive and compassionate that he robbed Louis of the competitive fire necessary to excel.

Correct answer: B. As I noted, Carl wasn't a perfect father, but he was always emotionally available when his son needed him, so they enjoyed a stable, secure relationship. This not only bolstered Louis's self-esteem, but it gave him the courage to fail. He found a career he loved, and, even though the odds of succeeding at it weren't high, he possessed the confidence necessary to focus on an ambitious goal and achieve it. Carl had the inner confidence as a father to support the differences between him and his son.

In real life, these three scenarios would, of course, be much more complex, but these are nonetheless fairly accurate. For the sake of making a point, I've simplified the actual causes and effects. You likely noticed the sometimes hidden, unobserved, or fully understood connection between a father's behaviors and an adult child's career decisions and work behaviors.

# Chapter 2

# CONNECTING
How Your Father's Attachment Style
Affects Your Relationships at Work

One of the first things in my life that I remember is standing in my crib and crying for my father. There are really no words that I can use to describe what I was feeling, but it was awful. Whenever I think of my childhood and my father, I start to feel frightened, and my fear turns into anger toward men. Where was my father? I know that my relationship with my father still affects me today.

—Debbie, age fifty-two (manager, mother, and twice divorced)

I knew growing up that my father was my safety net. I didn't know at the time, but he was always looking out for me. I have always had a sense that things will always work out and I will land on my feet. I know that my confidence and success professionally and personally are a result of my father always supporting and caring for me. There is no way I could be successful in business without my father's emotional support.

—Charles, age thirty-eight
(retail business owner, father, and married for five years)

People often ask me, what is the psychological secret to success in the business world? What is the one ingredient that they can use to "fast track" their careers and achieve ambitious goals? I always tell them that, from any perspective (business, legal, social, personal, and psychological), understanding the tremendous power and importance of relationships is the key. If you want to understand this power, then you need to grasp the concept of attachment, especially as it relates to your father. All relationships are based on attachment.

More specifically, you must be aware of the interplay that took place between you and your father in the early attachment process. As the word suggests, *attachment* involves the way in which you related to and bonded with your dad when you were growing up. The dictionary defines *attachment* as "a feeling that binds one person to another; devotion; with regard," which isn't a bad way of summarizing the concept. Without attachment, meaningful relationships would not exist. Attachment is our foundation for relating to the world, future partners, children, coworkers, customers, clients, supervisors, and ourselves. It is important to remember that we are wired genetically for relationships. One of the measurements of emotional and mental health is the ability to form and maintain relationships in all facets of your life.

I don't want to oversimplify the concept of attachment. Nor do I want to burden you with unnecessary psychological theory and jargon. Therefore, let's focus the discussion on the role that attachment plays in our development as human beings.

## A NATURAL RESPONSE: WHY WE REFLEXIVELY ATTACH

The pioneer of attachment research and theory is Dr. John Bowlby, a British psychiatrist who noted that no experiences "have more far reaching effects on personality development than . . . a child's experience within his family." The initial bonding experience with our father is the first place where we began to create a sense of who we are, especially in relationship to other people. Mothers and fathers are both critical to the bonding process. Holding, cuddling, and feeding are all critical to an infant's ability to feel safe and comfortable in the world. We naturally desire to connect, attach, and relate to the people in our world. *The attachment drive and the need for it* never diminishes *throughout our life*. Even when we are adults, the barometer of our mental and emotional health is always based on our ability to form meaningful attachments.[1]

According to Bowlby, our very first paternal (father-child) attachment has the power to create expectations about all our subsequent relationships.[2] This implies that, if we find our partner/lover as trustworthy or manipulative, our boss as supportive or demanding, our business associates as helpful or untrustworthy, these present-day experiences have their roots in the father-child relationship. More specifically, *how* we attached to our father affects our current relationships. It is of paramount importance to note that the attachment process with our mother is equally as critical. The impact of these early relationships can't be underestimated or dismissed. The paternal attachment process, however, tends to be overlooked, diminished, and the least understood. The reason for this cultural bias will be explained in the section on fathering styles. It is our focus here to better understand how your father's attachment style affected you and still influences your career today.

Understanding the nature of this attachment process provides us with often startling insights about our workplace behaviors and choices. If you look at leaders in organizations, you'll find that many of them came from homes where they had close relationships with strong fathers. Of course, you'll also find some leaders who had distant attachments with their fathers. The lack of emotional warmth caused this latter group to adopt a cold, aggressive leadership style—they tend to feel (unconsciously) that exhibiting emotion with subordinates would be unnatural. Similarly, some who had insecure attachments to their dads seek to work for bosses who are father substitutes—people who pay their subordinates a great deal of attention and exhibit a lot of empathy. There are also people who had such weak attachments to their fathers that they lack the self-esteem necessary to express themselves forcefully and creatively, which hurts them in their careers.

These are just a few of the many ways that attachment can have an impact on careers. Let's look at why attachment has such a powerful effect via two case histories.

Mary, thirty-six, is in the process of interviewing for a national director position with a Fortune 500 company. She has an advanced business degree, an excellent work history, the right job experience, and the support of her boss for a promotion. During the two-day interview, though, Mary has great difficulty making eye contact with the interviewing committee. Although she desperately wants to be liked and viewed as qualified for the position, she appears withdrawn and aloof. Mary feels that the hiring committee has already decided on another candidate and that the committee is just going through the motions.

What the hiring committee isn't aware of is Mary's habitual way of behaving when confronted with possible relationship changes and uncertainty. Faced with the prospect of losing old work relationships and having to form new ones, she becomes even more guarded than she normally is. Deep inside, Mary is convinced that other people don't find her likable and competent. Consequently, she retreats inward when she is placed in situations where people attempt to get to know her—for example, the hiring committee's interview process. Despite her prior success, Mary rationalizes away her accomplishments, telling herself that it's a combination of luck and a willingness to work hard. She's never looked deep inside herself to figure out the source of her nagging personal and professional insecurity.

When Mary came to me, though, we began this process of exploration, and we discovered that her father was severely depressed during most of her childhood. Her father would go to work, come home, sit on the couch, and read the evening newspaper without communicating with her or anyone else in the family. Mary never felt important to her father or that he really cared about her, and she had very little emotional contact or interaction with her father while growing up. As astonishing as it might seem, she doesn't recall her father ever asking her anything about her life—about her feelings or interests—until she was a senior in college. Even as an adult, Mary speaks to her father only when she calls him, which is usually about twice a year (his birthday and Thanksgiving).

Mary's natural human need for love, approval, and safety were not met by her dad. That's why her relationships at work have been so shaky and insecure. As she was growing up, she never had that inner core of emotional security and competence that a father can help a child acquire. Her father's voluntary emotional separation from her life made her feel that something was wrong with her. Despite her intelligence, skill, and work ethic, she still experiences that same lack of confidence, especially when she is faced with the possibility of significant change: the new position of national director. Until Mary understands and comes to terms with her attachment history and her father's style, she is going to be handicapped in work situations and never reach her potential. As you might expect, she didn't receive the promotion she wanted, but she is making progress in learning about how she related to her father. The critical insights she gleans will translate to how she views herself in the workplace and how she relates to her colleagues.

Mike, fifty-two, has a different attachment style with his father than Mary does, but the impact on his career is equally significant. Mike is a computer animation director for a major movie studio and develops scenes for each picture frame in the animated movie. This is very technical work and quite tedious. Mike recently lost his job as a result of his ongoing personality conflicts with other producers at the studio. The studio executives for whom Mike worked felt that he was talented but difficult to work with. Before he was fired, his boss encouraged Mike to become more of a team player and to be less focused on just getting the work completed. When Mike was fired, he was convinced that he was a victim of jealousy and age discrimination, that no one appreciated his creative computer animation talent.

When Mike came to see me, I asked him about his early childhood attachment with his father. Mike said, "While I was growing up, my father was rarely around the house because of my parents' divorce. I would see my father periodically and would enjoy our time together immensely, and then I would not see my father for long periods of time." Mike also explained that he would feel tremendously safe, happy, and content when he was in his father's presence. When he didn't see his father for weeks and sometimes months at a time, though, he would become depressed and would withdraw from his friends and family. His father's random absences forced Mike to grieve, and these powerful, confusing emotions at such a young age created a sense of insecurity. Mike said, "I was always surprised and glad to see my father again. I always thought he would never come back."

Based on these early attachments and detachments from his father, Mike preferred to keep an emotional distance from his supervisors and employees. His self-imposed isolation was a response to the ambivalence and sadness of his relationship with his father. Precisely because he loved the time spent with his dad, it was terribly painful when he was absent for long stretches. To protect himself, Mike chose to maintain an "icy" (how colleagues described him) persona at work. Interestingly, Mike was warm and caring in his close personal relationships. His father's legacy wasn't all bad; the time he spent with Mike really was quality time; he taught Mike the value of intimacy and communication in relationships.

For Mike to demonstrate this human side in his work relationships, he must learn to cope with the emotional disconnections and connections that naturally occur during the course of business. Employees resign or are fired; bosses get promoted and transferred; customers come and go; disagreements with team members occur; movie projects start and finish, and so on. Mike must separate his early paternal attachment history from his present-day work relationships. I'm helping him see how the duality of his relationship with his father is mirrored in his personal and professional relationships. He needs to get his arms around the natural experiences of making connections and then having disconnections. The way in which Mike enjoyed a great relationship with his dad when he was around has translated into the great relationships he enjoys in his personal life. Similarly, when his dad wasn't around, he was withdrawn and depressed, and he shows the same negative reactions when faced with work-relationship changes. Acknowledging this duality and making a serious, consistent effort to being aware of how he shuts others out will help him overcome the relationship problems that have plagued him and derailed his entire career.

## WHAT ATTACHMENT ISSUES ARE CAUSING YOU PROBLEMS AT WORK?

It's possible that you had a strong, positive attachment with your father, in which case your career has probably benefited. The odds are, however, that your relationship was a mixed bag at best. Most fathers a generation or two ago didn't know as much about being a father as we know today, and, as a result, they often didn't form the type of close relationships with their children that dads are more likely to form now.

*The good news is that, no matter what type of attachment you had, you can overcome its negative effect.* The first step in reversing the damage is to determine your vulnerability. To do so, place a check next to the behaviors that apply to you. The first set of behaviors relate to work; the second set involve your father. As you look over this list below, be aware that a given behavior is worthy of a check if it represents a recurring theme or pattern in your life; you don't have to exhibit this behavior all the time and your father didn't have to act in a given way on a daily basis.

*Attachment Issues*

\_\_\_\_ Have difficulty trusting and connecting emotionally with colleagues, supervisors, suppliers, and clients/customers.

\_\_\_\_ Are emotionally aloof and removed from others in the workplace.

\_\_\_\_ Experience problems developing and maintaining positive "people skills."

___ Have difficulty with any type of emotional endings and/or changes in the workplace (farewells, terminations, transfers, business-plan changes).

___ Display ambivalence about forming long-term professional relationships.

___ Have difficulty showing and expressing empathy toward colleagues, bosses, customers, or vendors.

___ Exhibit a tendency to be either clingy and/or aggressive when under work stress.

___ Extremely competitive with colleagues to such an extent that it is damaging to your career.

___ Have personality problems with bosses and other work authority figures (this includes any work hierarchy structure).

___ Feel insecure about your job, your job performance, and/or your colleagues.

___ Choose jobs or assignments that don't challenge you.

___ Deliberately avoid any type of positive emotional expression with colleagues, bosses, or clients.

## Father Issues

___ Father was often emotionally unavailable during your childhood.

___ Father was often physically absent during your childhood.

___ Father exhibited only anger when upset or frustrated. All other emotions weren't expressed.

___ Father had no close friends or close relationships at work.

___ Father rarely expressed positive emotions, especially with you.

___ Father was inconsistent in his relationship with you (sometimes there, sometimes not, both emotionally and physically).

___ Father often seemed sad or depressed when you were around.

___ Father didn't have much energy and usually didn't engage in activities with you.

___ Father was passively involved in your life growing up. He didn't know much about you, your interests, or your friends.

___ Father never expressed personal satisfaction or pride about his career.

If you have no checks in either section, you probably enjoyed a secure attachment with your father, and attachment issues aren't likely to affect your career negatively (though other aspects of his fathering style might have, which I'll address in chapters 4–8). If you had only one or two checks in each section, then attachment issues may affect on your career but don't appear to be an issue. If you have three or more checks in each section, the odds are that you have significant attachment issues that are currently causing major career problems. Attachment issues might be one of the reasons that your career has stalled. However, your career can always be revived and redirected through a new understanding of attachment.

Obviously, some of the traits on the checklist could result from other factors besides the father factor, but my goal here isn't to deliver a definitive diagnosis as much as to get you thinking about these important issues concerning career relationships. Most of us don't consider how we attached with our father, and, even if we do, we're unlikely to relate it to our own attachment style in the workplace or our career difficulties. This checklist is just a way to start making mental connections and to begin making sense of these seemingly disparate behaviors. There is a direct correlation between your success and frustration and your father-daughter or father-son relationship.

If you have a number of checks on each list, don't despair or consider your relationship with your father to be worthless or hopeless. The odds are that you, like most people, have some degree of successful attachment with your father. "Attachment" is on a continuum that ranges from nonexistent to secure and consistent, and you're probably somewhere in the middle. As shaky or sporadic as your child-father relationship may have been, you probably also enjoyed times where your father was there for you emotionally, physically, and mentally.

Remember, too, that what's past is past. *Your life is in front of you, not behind you.* Your concern now is what you can do to improve your career prospects and job performance. Fortunately, there's a lot you can do. Whatever the quality of your attachment might have been, you can use it to make better choices about work today and in the future. To help you do so, let's define your particular type of attachment based on the following four styles: *intermittent, avoidant, depressed,* and *secure.* Each style has its very own characteristics and approach that affect one's childhood and adulthood. The question that you need to answer is: Could the attachment style I had with my father still be a hindrance in my career? It is important for you to gain valuable career insight into yourself and use it to change your present and future professional path.

# INTERMITTENT STYLE

As the name implies, the intermittent style of relating is hit or miss, random, and inconsistent. Sometimes kids have their emotional (love, support, concern), physical (food, shelter), and mental (eye contact, talking) needs met. Other times, dads don't address these primary needs. It is these misses in life from birth to age ten that shape a young person's experience of the world. If a young girl comes home from school with tears in her eyes and her father doesn't notice or, worse, notices but doesn't ask what is wrong, this young girl will begin to feel unimportant. If this neglect continues, she'll not only feel unimportant but also begin to act as if her actions are of no particular consequence.

What really does have an impact on you as a child, though, is that Dad sometimes notices the tears and offers comfort. He responds appropriately, and you feel loved, cared for, and safe. Unfortunately, the next three times you are feeling scared, depressed, or excited, your father might not respond in this positive manner. This uncertainty and inconsistent fathering feeds a child's fear that the world isn't a safe place. Emotional consistency and predictability builds trust, and trust is the foundation for all attachments and relationships in a child's and an adult's life. Without trust, it is almost impossible to form any type of functional career relationships. The far end of this attachment style is the formation of a paranoid personality. These are the sons or daughters who assume that everyone is out to get them and no one can be trusted. Paranoia to any degree in the workplace is a true hindrance to your career development, professional satisfaction, and advancement.

Some dads are infrequently inconsistent, while others are always this way. Children of the latter type tend not only to distrust others but also to suspect that good things won't happen for them. Consistent dads, on the other hand, help us feel secure in the world and allow us to trust others. They demonstrate that they know how we feel, so we come to expect this from our dads. Their sensitivity and caring allows us to go out into the world with self-confidence.

How does a father's inconsistent attachment style affect an adult child's career and workplace behaviors?

First, this individual tends to be wary of others. If he's a boss, he rarely levels with his subordinates, feeling that there is such a thing as "on a need-to-know basis" and that his people usually don't need to know everything.

This individual often has problems on teams, keeping his ideas to himself, and is unwilling to let others share in the credit when an idea works. Second, the child of inconsistent attachment might receive a performance report that notes how she can't always be counted on to deliver and that she acts like a different person on different days—sometimes she's friendly and works hard, while other days she's sullen and gets little done. Third, this person is often pessimistic and cynical and usually interprets events negatively. Employers often consider this individual incapable of motivating others or being a leader in the workplace.

Joan, who had an inconsistent attachment with her father, is a very talented software designer who quit her job with a top software company to start her own firm. She had a terrific software product and received significant backing from a venture capital firm. Her company, however, floundered—in no small part because of Joan's inability to keep good people and establish solid work relationships with customers. She alienated the former by micromanaging their work and the latter with her negative attitude. Joan, though, didn't "get it" or believe she had any role in her company's struggle. In fact, the high turnover rate in her company and her losing a major customer reinforced her pessimistic, unsafe view of the world.

To assess whether you, like Joan, are being affected now by an inconsistent attachment you had with your father, consider the following questions:

1. Do you find it difficult to trust people in your career?
2. Who is the main person in your career whom you trust and are emotionally connected with (other than yourself)?
3. Do you know or suspect that the person you trust has any idea that she's your main confidante?
4. Do you feel that your attitude and actions toward your colleagues vary considerably depending on the mood you're in; if you've ever received 360-degree feedback from them, have they noted that they never know which "you" will show up?
5. Do you believe that you'll never fulfill your career goals; do you treat each setback as a catastrophic event?
6. Do you withdraw emotionally from coworkers when you are upset, sad, stressed, or excited?
7. Do you tend to avoid any or all emotional types of connections with your coworkers?

Connecting   49
8. When you make an emotional attachment or connection at work, do you worry about it or regret doing it later?

The more yes answers, the more likely that you're being influenced by the inconsistent attachment style of your father. The wisdom and beauty of insight is using it to change your present-day concerns and behaviors and making better choices.

## AVOIDANT STYLE

With the avoidant attachment style, the father lacks emotional expression, physical contact, and outward empathic communication. Hugging, hand holding, kissing, and other nurturing types of behaviors aren't part of this style. Adult children use words such as "cold," "aloof," "emotionally distant," and "unable to express love" to describe these dads. Of course, nearly all these men love their sons and daughters, but they have difficulty expressing their love verbally, empathetically, or through any degree of demonstration. As a result, many of their children become accustomed to emotional isolation and learn to cope with life's ups and downs on their own rather than by sharing their feelings or thoughts with others. When they become scared, stressed, or upset, they're more likely to retreat into themselves rather than seek solace from family and friends. Isolation is this daughter's or son's safe place in a crisis.

As adults, children of avoidant fathers similarly detach themselves from others in the workplace. Emotional expression still makes them uncomfortable, so they rarely become angry with others and are likely to change the subject if a colleague or subordinate starts talking angrily about a boss or coworker. They have trouble making or maintaining relationships that rely on emotional disclosure or connection. For this reason, they often aren't very good with clients and customers; they are perceived as "paper pushers," "bureaucrats," and "functionaries," and their emotional neutrality is sometimes mistaken for a lack of interest and involvement in the work and the coworkers around them. As managers, they usually turn "people problems" over to human resources rather than deal with them on their own. While these individuals can generate great concrete results and may be superb individual contributors, their lack of people skills imposes an artificial career ceiling. These sons and daughters have tremendous difficulty with human relationships and emotional interactions on any deep level. This is a major roadblock for any career ascension and development.

Another concern resulting from the father's avoidant attachment style is that daughter or son is commonly viewed as a loner, recluse, or outsider in the emotional atmosphere of the company/workplace. This lack of emotional connection and reluctance to be emotionally vulnerable is a major impairment for any significant career growth. People don't respond well to a customer, colleague, or supervisor who is emotionally aloof and distant. Confidence, trust, and career development is built around close human connections, and avoidant children and adults don't like these types of dealings.

Joe, for instance, grew up with a dad who was an accountant. Joe said that his father seemed to measure his children with the same cold, calculating eye that he used on client audits. Joe remembers his dad hugging him only once as a child—at the funeral of Joe's own father. He hasn't followed in his father's footsteps—he makes it a point to hug his children and express his love for them regularly. Yet he finds it very difficult to warm up to people at work. Joe works for a large New York public relations firm, but his primary responsibilities are "back room" duties—writing press releases, mass e-mail letters, and speeches; creating media strategies; and so on. His firm values his skills, but they know he doesn't interact very well with people—with either clients or reporters—so he's achieved only modest success in his field. For years, Joe was convinced that his lack of advancement was because of his excellent writing and media-analysis skills; he figured that his firm didn't want to promote him to a managerial position where he would no longer be able to use these skills full time on behalf of the firm. He's only recently started to understand that the real issue is how he reflexively pushes people away when they get too close, how he shuts down conversations with others, especially when people become upset or even overly excited about an accomplishment.

Has your father's avoidant style of attachment caused or contributed to your work-related problems? The following questions will help you explore these issues further:

1. Do you prefer to work independently? Do you find collaborating difficult or a waste of time?
2. Do you have anyone in your office to which you can open up to emotionally about job-related problems and career concerns?

3. When you're under stress on the job, do you find yourself avoiding expressing how you feel about stressful situations (e.g., sharing your fears concerning losing your job in the upcoming downsizing, a missed deadline, or a negative personnel encounter)?
4. Do you believe that no one at work knows the real you?
5. When a colleague comes to you in tears or in anger, do you immediately try to shut off the emotion and focus only on the facts?
6. When you're with people who are talking empathetically about colleagues who have been fired or passed over for a promotion, do you try to change the subject to a more emotionally neutral topic?
7. Even if you have a good job and have done reasonably well at it, do you feel empty and unfulfilled?
8. Do you avoid any degree of emotional expression about your own career with your closest friend at work?
9. Do you perceive yourself as the type of man or woman who is comfortable with his or her own emotions and the emotions and opinions of others?

Again, the more yes answers, the greater the likelihood that your father's avoidant attachment style affects you at work.

## DEPRESSED STYLE

While your father may not have been clinically depressed (unable to function on daily basis in all areas), he may have had little energy, acted distracted, and wasn't particularly responsive to your needs. He may not have been like this all the time, but his depressed attachment style may have kicked in when he lost a job or experienced some other financial setback. A depressed attachment style may also have been because of illness, substance abuse, or a problematic attachment history with his father. Whether his depressed mood was based on outside events or was chronic, it likely communicated a lack of interest in you. Children don't realize that their dad's own unhappiness or depression has nothing to do with them. Through the eyes of children, this father seems unresponsive because of them. Typically, children will personalize their father's behavior as a result of what they do or say. As a result, they suffer self-esteem problems and may try to compensate by acting out or by retreating into a shell (because nothing they do is worthy of notice).

A typical example of this attachment style goes like this. A daughter comes home from preschool with a finger painting and presents it to her father. He looks at it, sets it down, perhaps nods, but never compliments or thanks her or interacts with her or her work of art. This daughter learns at an early age that she isn't important and her efforts are beneath notice. This assumption is incorrect, toxic, and developmentally debilitating. Consequently, this child will grow up having to deal with significant issues of emotional neglect and abandonment. If a child doesn't deal with them by the time he or she reaches adulthood, the repercussions will be constantly felt in the workplace.

No matter how much we accomplish in school or in our careers, we possess a core need to feel valued and cherished by our parents. If your father was depressed, ambivalent, or distracted and didn't show how much he valued you when you were young, you internalized the feeling of not being wanted. Later, it may surface as nagging doubts about your self-worth, a feeling that others don't like you, and what you do isn't all that important. As adults, these individuals may also feel shame for not being worthy of notice. This nagging feeling of not being "good enough" is a very powerful deterrent to a positive career path.

In jobs, this particular attachment style causes people to meet their emotional needs through salary advancement, job titles, and work goals rather than through relationships. Ironically, this focus often causes them to fall short of their career objectives because they don't come across as confident or decisive. Internal doubts about self-worth, shame (the exaggerated feeling of being defective), and insecurity about making the right choice all hinder them professionally.

Anne, for instance, was passed over twice for senior management openings in her corporation despite a brilliant work record as an individual contributor. Anne didn't impress the management committee of her company as "leadership material." It wasn't because she was a woman; the organization's CEO was a woman. Instead, it was the perception that Anne was indecisive and a poor personnel motivator. The feedback Anne received was that, even when she had a great idea or was presenting a terrific strategy, she was almost apologetic about it, that she would voice her own concerns about the flaws in a strategy rather than convince others of its strengths.

If the results of a depressed attachment style sound familiar, see whether the following workplace responses apply to you:

- Do you experience feelings of shame for no apparent reason when under job stress?
- If you've achieved a measure of success in your job or your career, do you still feel like a fraud, as if you've hoodwinked everyone into thinking you're competent?
- Do you avoid taking professional risks because of your fear of failing or looking incompetent?
- Do you have difficulty accepting compliments, suspecting others are just giving you strokes because of your position or because they want something from you?
- In the middle of a meeting or when sitting at your desk, do you suddenly feel terribly sad without any specific cause?
- Do you underestimate your abilities, influence, and significance to others in the office?
- Do you sometimes daydream about becoming really important and successful so that everyone will appreciate you at work?

These questions are designed to point out that you might have a depressed style of relating to yourself and the people surrounding your career. A father's depressed attachment style tends to breed personal depression in the son or daughter. Personal depression can be a significant roadblock to your career growth. (See chapter 6 to learn more about depressed fathering styles.)

## SECURE STYLE

The secure style is the ideal attachment style, one characterized by being able to emotionally read, listen to, and learn about a child's needs. This kind of father is consistent in meeting the early needs (physical, emotional, and mental) of his children in such a manner that they learn to trust him. This early bond of trust and safety is the foundation for all future personality development, intellectual growth, and professional choices.

Securely attached children learn that they are important in the world because of the constant attention, concern, and loving gestures extended to them by their father. While the vast majority of kids receive some of these positive demonstrations no matter what their father's attachment style is, it is often sporadic. Consistency is crucial so that children generally know they can expect love and support from their dads. Certainly conflict and other problems are part of the father-child relationship, but even when there are tension and fights, the child knows with certainty that her dad loves her; she never loses her trust in him, even if she's furious because he grounds her for bad grades. This child naturally develops inner strength and emotional resources.

As a result of this attachment style, these children grow up to excel in jobs and reach ambitious career goals. They have the capacity to emotionally connect, take risks, be empathic, trust coworkers, and help foster a sense of belongingness. They project an air of confidence and decisiveness that makes them logical candidates for management and leadership positions. They function effectively even during crises, drawing on a strong sense of self to remain calm in the midst of chaos. They also recognize how much their coworkers, employees, and clients crave to have a secure attachment and relationship with the people around them, and they make an effort to form and facilitate these relationships.

Bill's father, for instance, had a secure attachment style. Though Bill's father was not particularly wealthy or successful, his fathering style was in no small part responsible for Bill's becoming a CEO of a large commercial construction corporation. Bill went to a state school, was a good but not spectacular student, and lacked the type of professional connections that many other future CEOs enjoyed. But he was rapidly promoted in a series of jobs and selected for the top spot because, in the words of his company's CEO selection committee, "he can do it all." Bill demonstrated a skill for getting things done throughout his career, but, most important, he also exhibited strong values in line with his company's culture. He was astute when it came to finances, but he also focused his time and attention on building relationships within the company and with customers and suppliers. He also was willing to take "educated risks," helping the company capitalize on opportunities that a more conservative executive would never have seized upon. At the same time, Bill never took foolish risks. In short, he was the type of focused, confident, competent leader that all companies want but often don't find.

Did your father have a secure attachment style with you? See how you respond to the following work-related questions:

- Do you offer emotional support in the workplace to your colleagues consistently?

- Do you feel as if your colleagues trust you; are they willing to share with you fears, doubts, and complaints that they would not share with a less trustworthy person?
- Do you believe you take reasonable risks to capitalize on business opportunities; can you name two or three risks you've taken in recent years that have paid off for your organization?
- In performance peer reviews and from feedback you've received from your supervisors, are you considered decisive?
- Are you a good networker? Have you built strong relationships within and outside of your company that have helped you achieve business goals?
- Do you find personal and professional strength from your relationships at work?

The more yes answers you have, the better. Even if your relationship with your father was lacking, it is possible to move your management style and your relationship style with others in a more favorable direction. The steps below and throughout this book outline how to turn your father factor into a positive force in your career in order to maximize your potential. The first step is to recognize your father's particular attachment style (chapters 4–8) and what rules you live by that derive from your father (chapter 9). Once you have discerned these two things, change not only is possible but will create a welcomed relief.

## HOW UNDERSTANDING ATTACHMENT HELPS YOU IN YOUR CAREER

Attachments are just one piece of the father factor puzzle, but they make up an important piece. Being aware of your father's attachment style and its impact on your workplace behaviors isn't going to solve all your career problems, but it can provide valuable insights that can be the start of a positive solution. I've found that people are routinely amazed to discover that the roadblocks faced in every job they've had can frequently be obliterated when they understand the principles of attachment. Just being aware of your vulnerabilities because your father had an intermittent attachment style, for instance, gives you a way to manage this problem.

The odds are that you can now identify the attachment style you grew up with. Given that style, here are some ideas and things to do that can counteract its negative effects.

## Intermittent

- Keep a journal of five new career behaviors, with the goal of practicing them consistently. This may include keeping appointments, returning phone calls in a timely manner, following up on business leads, making a lunch appointment with a colleague, and finishing assignments ahead of schedule.
- Practice complimenting people at work for their efforts, even if it feels phony or awkward. Make a point each day for one week to notice and acknowledge something that an employee, colleague, or client has done of which you approve. Take a risk and verbalize your appreciation of your coworkers.
- Make a list of people you want to follow up with, especially those who have expressed concerns or requested assistance. Overcome your impulse to put these issues on the back burner, hoping they disappear. You don't have to solve everyone's problems, but you owe it to them to check on their progress, provide them updates, and support and answer their questions. Following up is a powerful way of conveying to people that you care about their concerns and efforts.

## Avoidant

- Make a list of your "emotional exchange capacity." This means that you note occasions when you share laughter with your colleagues, express anger or fear relating to work situations, and show happiness or satisfaction with a work task or career move. If you find you're recording few or no emotional exchanges, make a conscious effort to make one. Start with a small emotional exchange once a week for a month, and then try twice a week the next month. Gradually, this will help you establish and strengthen relationships.
- Keep a journal of your feelings and thoughts in work situations. Describe a situation and why you felt a certain way and what you thought about your reactions. Each entry should be at least one page.

This exercise will help you get in touch with your emotions and make them feel "safer." Once you express them on paper, it's often easier to express them verbally.

- When a colleague, client, or supervisor makes an emotional expression to you, acknowledge it and try to respond in like manner. Focus on being emotionally receptive in the workplace. This step requires you to think of questions that involve someone's feelings and emotions.
- Make a point at least once a day to start a sentence with "I feel . . ." about your work situation, clients, and personal relationships. This deliberate statement of feeling can start to unlock your emotional capacity and ability.

## Depressed

- Increase the time you spend interacting with people on a meaningful level at work; make an effort through lunches, private conversations, and after-work activities to establish relationships that go beyond surface exchanges of information; shift a significant percentage of your e-mail communication and phone interactions to in-person conversations.
- Track your accomplishments; keep a written "achievement" journal where you list small and large goals that your efforts helped achieve; note specific compliments from others—bosses, subordinates, customers, suppliers—and what skills or qualities of yours they were praising.
- Don't allow yourself to remain isolated from your coworkers. Take deliberate steps to have more face-to-face interactions with your clients and coworkers. This might mean walking upstairs to another office to answer a question.
- When you think you're isolating yourself at work, make a date or appointment and go talk to someone about your frustration. This step will put you into the inner loop in the office. People bond when issues are discussed on an emotional level. You need to reach out to people and get out of your emotional "cave."

You can also use this information about the psychology of attachments to examine how you relate to others in the workplace. Some people find that their attachment style mirrors that of their fathers, while others discover that their style of relating is the opposite of their dads' style. Obviously, striving for a secure style of relating with colleagues makes sense, but most of us display a mixture of secure and insecure styles. We may, for instance, have secure attachments with subordinates and an avoidant style with bosses. Take a moment and determine your attachment style with the following:

- bosses
- subordinates
- peers
- customers/clients
- suppliers

It may be that a particular type of person pushes you into a counterproductive style of attachment. Bosses, in particular, represent father figures for many people and may trigger negative behaviors. I've counseled many people who had great relationships with the four other types of individuals listed above but reflexively related to their bosses as they did to their fathers. I've also known people who had strong, secure relationships with bosses but had problems with subordinates—or customers, peers, or suppliers. Human relationships are complex, and the attachment styles at one's job mirror this complexity. There is a twofold myth: that work relationships don't matter (only profits do) and that our baseline for these career relationships didn't start with our father (I am independent of my relationship with my father).

I don't expect you to execute a 180-degree turnaround, an overnight change in your attachment style. I do expect you to be aware of the attachment issues raised here and that you'll be open to considering change. Keep in mind that even small, positive changes in your attachment style can pay major dividends. Displaying a little more confidence when dealing with bosses or a dollop of empathy when talking to subordinates can have a positive influence on your job performance and career prospects.

To work toward secure attachments, remember that everyone in your professional life (as well as everyone in your personal life, for that matter) has the same need for the big five elements of a relationship: *trust, a sense of belonging, concern, security, and love*. Remember, too, that relationships compose the foundation for all professional growth. Whatever amount of time, energy, and change you put into improving the quality of your relationships and attachments, it is time well spent and will reap huge benefits today and in the future.

Chapter 3

# WHAT YOU CAN DO ABOUT IT

How Knowledge and Insight Give You Power over
Your Career Choices and Job Performance

I never seem to get the promotion or credit that I deserve. It always seems
that someone else gets it—I feel very ignored and not noticed at work. It
seems very unfair, but something I have to learn to live with.

—Jane, age forty-five

My father was a workaholic. He worked six days a week and traveled six
months out of the year. Now, I find myself doing the same thing, and it isn't
getting me ahead in my personal life. I barely see my kids, and my wife
makes appointments to see me at work. My boss loves my commitment, but
it is killing me, and I don't see what I can change.

—Mike, age thirty-six

W e have discussed how understanding your father factor in the
workplace is of paramount importance. This seldom understood
and applied concept is the big secret to becoming empowered and to succeeding with your professional and personal goals. By understanding your
relationship with your father, you can gain practical information that you can
use for your career. The key is to begin to grasp your father's legacy. The
type of change, both professionally and personally, is attainable by using
your father factor to your advantage. The problem, many times, is that the
minor issues and behaviors in your career are the ball and chain that hold you
back from that promotion, the new opportunity you desire. The solutions and

changes that you want seem always to elude you. It feels as if there really isn't anything besides a miracle or an act of God that could change your work and career circumstances. The same old problems, issues, and frustrations keep reappearing. To use an old saying, what's the white elephant in the room you're ignoring? Your father factor is the huge white elephant in many of these seemingly dead-end career situations.

Regardless of your situation, you will see that there are legitimate changes that can be implemented to move your career to the next level. First, we have to understand these problems, identify them, and consider the possibility of proactive change. Then, we can begin to see the invaluable role that the father factor plays in these seemingly unrelated career issues. It is all too common to step over and ignore your relationship with your father, particularly if you weren't close to him or never had a father.

In the following five chapters, I am going to discuss the various fathering styles and how each has it strengths and weaknesses for a person in the workplace. In this chapter, it is important to start making some emotional and mental connections between how your career is evolving, its roadblocks, and your goals and your father.

We have already examined in the last two chapters how your attachments in relationships—both personal and professional—have their origins with your father. Here I am going to illustrate the direct relationship between many of the problems you encounter at work and their roots in your father-daughter or father-son relationship. These seemingly endless issues or minor irritations can be changed if properly understood. Change is the goal of this entire book—along with how to use your father's legacy to further your professional success and satisfaction.

We are going to explore seven of the most common problems in the workplace that might seem unrelated to your father factor but, in fact, are. There are profound emotional, mental, and unconscious connections to your father that often manifest themselves as professional conflicts, career roadblocks, and nagging self-doubts. The practical solutions can be better understood once you consciously recognize that these problems can be addressed and aren't beyond the hand of change.

As a psychologist, I have often found in my professional experience that 80 percent of a career problem is the mere recognition of it, and only 20 percent is the proactive change. The emotional resistance and psychological denial that lead to avoidant behaviors are the major stumbling blocks that affect even the most conscientious professionals. These sophisticated emotional defense mechanisms can get in the way of effective change, limiting your potential and thwarting your professional goals. The aim of this chapter is to make the unconscious self-defeating, self-limiting behaviors conscious. Once these behaviors are exposed and recognized, then changes can be implemented. Insight leads to change in psychology and all human behavior. Without insight and without making these important conscious connections, your career roadblocks will likely remain in place.

The concept of change may not be a new one, but adaptability in the workplace is now more critical than ever. *Your* father factor—meaning the particular critical influence your father had on you, which has translated into your behavior and style—may need to be adjusted in order to achieve success. To be proficient at problem solving, an individual must develop cognitive, emotional, and intellectual abilities to begin to see below the surface of a problem or issue. Many times a critical attitude, a negative belief, or a particular behavior is at the root of a problem in the work environment. Often, these negative belief systems are deeply rooted in the past and were never recognized as limiting. Gaining insight into these old beliefs, without blaming your father or condemning your family history, will bring to you the psychological tools necessary to create change in your career—and in your life.

## THE BIG SEVEN FATHER FACTOR ISSUES IN ALL CAREERS

Some of the most common personnel and career issues in the workplace are shame, self-doubt, lack of focus, lack of motivation, lack of personal responsibility, emotional immaturity, and fear of failure. These seven common workplace problems are found in all levels and areas of the business world, in both the private and public sectors. They occur far and wide: in the family business, in corporate boardrooms, in public schools, in the military, in professional sports, in government and city offices, in sales and marketing, in the entertainment industry, and in the medical and legal fields. No profession is spared from having individuals struggling with one or more of these seven common behaviors that produce roadblocks. The key question again is: can you begin to understand and recognize your own roadblocks in the workplace?

Many psychological tests attempt to measure these problems, but they often fall short and miss the mark. A paper-and-pencil test doesn't always yield the type of information that is necessary for each individual to understand his or her life or career. *Rather, emotional and mental recognition— gained through probing questions and insights—expose self-defeating behaviors and beliefs that may change the course of a person's career and life.* Let's take a look at two professional real-life stories of highly functioning, successful individuals in their respective careers, both unaware of the negative impact their father factor had on them.

## JANE'S AND MIKE'S STORIES

For example, Jane, whose quotation began the chapter, is one of four children, the youngest in her family. While growing up, Jane frequently felt left out and overlooked by her successful business executive father. As an adult, Jane has gone through a series of different jobs with her company and has always felt underappreciated and undervalued. This inner self-doubt and shame has been nagging at her as long as she can remember. Unfortunately, she has set up her career in such a way that her unconscious actions reflect this self-doubt and low self-esteem. However, she has begun to recognize that she speaks and acts in a manner that reflects her lack of worth in the workplace.

Jane will constantly make self-deprecating comments about her quality of work, her leadership abilities, and her appearance to her colleagues and supervisors. Her sense of humor is very dark, far too personal, and full of self-loathing comments. Coworkers think she is very funny and quick witted. Still, Jane readily admits that she doesn't have a strong professional sense of herself in the workplace, which drives her constant sense of professional insecurity. She will never apply or volunteer for any assignment that is new or unfamiliar to her. She feels that she has painted herself into a career corner. Jane, through therapy and by following the steps in the second half of this book, is starting to explore the dynamics of her father-daughter relationship. She is beginning to see that the connection between her father's emotional neglect of her as a child and the resulting deep pain that she experienced has an impact on her life and career today. On a personal level, Jane has married and divorced twice and has always dated men twenty years her senior. These very obvious patterns of shame, self-doubt, and emotional immaturity are directly connected to the style of fathering she grew up with.

Jane's story may seem very basic to illustrate a point, but don't be deceived. The essential thing to remember is that Jane has been operating under these clouded, confusing career issues based on her father factor for the last twenty-five years, and that is a complex matter. She is so accustomed to them that they feel like part of her personality and beyond the hand of change. Jane, in reality, is a very successful professional woman, a self-supporting single mother, and physically active. Jane doesn't see anything else in her life but the deep sense of neglect in the back of her mind. Her dad's style of fathering was passive—there but not there (discussed in detail in chapter 6). Now that Jane is beginning to address her big three professional and personal issues of shame, self-doubt, and emotional immaturity along with her dad's style of fathering for the first time, Jane's career and sense of self are changing in a positive direction.

Jane has wondered for years why she has always found a way to passively sabotage her forward career movement at exactly the right moment with her supervisors, clients, and coworkers. For example, she inadvertently will forget to call a new client back, will skip a deadline, or will miss a critical planning meeting right before a potential promotion. These behaviors have all reinforced her inner personal issues of shame, self-doubt, and emotional immaturity. Now that she is finally connecting the dots by seeing the underlying patterns from the perspective of the father factor, she is finding that her career growth now looks very positive. Jane doesn't feel that her professional behavior will continue to lead her back to the seemingly dead end that she's sick of. The infamous glass ceiling for Jane was her own choices and unresolved father factor issues.

Mike's career story is just as interesting as Jane's, but with some very different issues. I met Mike because he is a workaholic, and his wife gave him an ultimatum to become more involved in the family, or she and the kids were leaving him. Mike didn't believe Marla at first until she took their two boys and moved out of their house unannounced. This was after a ten-day business trip that Mike had promised his wife he wouldn't take. He came home and found a note on the kitchen counter stating that, unless he stopped trying to gain his father's approval and became more involved in the family, he wasn't going to have one. Well, the premeditated crisis worked and got Mike to stop and look at his deep-seated fear of failure. Mike knew he had some unresolved emotional issues with his father, which were driving him to a point of professional and personal crisis. He admits that he knew his obsession with work and achievement wasn't normal and was far too consuming, especially compared with that of his colleagues and the board of directors.

Mike has been driven by the need to succeed for as long as he can remember. His father, Stan, worked around the clock, according to Mike, and was rarely home during the week. Mike's mother always told him and his two brothers that their father had an important career that demanded all his attention. But Mike still missed his father's love and support and never remembers Stan coming to his elementary, middle, or high school for any event (sports included) or special occasion. Mike knew that his father was very successful professionally and financially. This allowed the family to move several times. Each move was into a more expensive neighborhood with bigger houses and nicer cars. Stan always told Mike that these nice things in life don't come without hard work or a price. Mike recalls that his mother knew the trade-off for her husband's professional success, which was his absence from the family. Mike is also painfully aware that his father believed that, unless you ran the company or owned it, you were a "loser."

Stan was also very critical of the grades that Mike and his brothers received in school. If they didn't get A's, there was hell to pay when Stan came home on the weekend. Stan was very intolerant of any effort that wasn't perfect or the top grade in the class. Even though Mike rarely saw his father while growing up, his dad's critical superachiever attitudes hovered like a dark rain cloud over the entire family. Mike once came home from summer school with a B– in English. Stan blew up, called Mike an "idiot and a loser," and grounded him for the rest of the summer. Mike had to read seven American classic novels by September 1 or face the anger and disappointment of his father. So Mike strived to achieve some degree of success in school, sports, or any competition to gain his father's attention and love. Those brief moments of acceptance, genuine concern, and approval from Stan were very few and far between in Mike's childhood and adult life. When Mike graduated from a prestigious business school with an MBA, all Stan could say was, "Now maybe you can finally make something of yourself and make some serious money like I did." Even to this day, Stan has retired to Florida and will always ask Mike about his career and business first and rarely about his grandchildren or his wife.

Mike, unlike his brothers, chose to become the "perfect son" and always tried to gain his father's approval through professional success and accomplishments. Mike's two other brothers are both classic underachievers and have had great difficulty in the workplace. Stan has no relationship with Mike's two brothers because of their poor work ethic and below-average career performance. Mike has taken his father's constant need for success and developed it into his own career pattern. He is employed in the communication technology part of the company where he is a vice president and works a minimum of sixty-five hours a week, including one weekend day. Mike is very critical of his colleagues who don't exhibit the same work ethic or time commitment. He is rather pushy, money obsessed, and intolerant of any degree of emotional expression in the workplace. He has been criticized more than once by a peer for a lack of compassion and empathy in the company for his employees and colleagues. Mike, much like Stan, is emotionally avoidant and lacks insight into people and the complexities of life.

Mike knows that his inner insecurity, fear of failure, and sense of shame about not being "good enough" have driven him to the point that he can't work any more hours to offset these nagging issues. Mike has to finally address, examine, and feel his unresolved issues concerning his father factor. By experiencing the shock and real-life prospect of losing his family, and by facing a painful divorce (all divorces are painful regardless of the circumstances), he is coming to terms with his own father factor issues and is changing. Mike now realizes that he is "good enough" and that the workplace isn't the place to resolve his father and son issues. The more that he realizes the impact of his father on his career and professional and personal relationships, the more power he will have to change the direction of his life. Mike is overcoming Stan's superachiever style of fathering with new insight and new action. (See chapter 4 for more on the superachiever style of fathering.)

Mike and Jane have both had to come face-to-face with the big seven father factor issues in the workplace and realize that their own professional and personal satisfaction are directly related to the outcome. Now let us do a diagnostic check of the father factor issues in your career that might be undiagnosed or improperly understood. The definitions and checklists of the big seven issues are designed to help you begin to see the threads and patterns of problems that recur in your career and personal relationships. If you are going to make any significant, lasting change, the first step is to be aware of these problems and really understand that they are rooted in your relationship with your father. Unfortunately, *most people skip this step and think that their father is a nonissue.* I recommend that you take another serious look at him.

## THE FATHER FACTOR CHECKLIST: WHAT'S HAPPENING WITH YOU?

The following list of the big seven father factor issues is designed to give you a working model of some of the more typical behavioral patterns associated with each psychological problem. Unless you begin to emotionally, mentally, and psychologically look at these issues, it will be extremely difficult to make any life, career, or personal changes. Be honest with yourself if any of these issues might relate to you and could possibly describe how you handle certain situations concerning work, clients, and authority figures. It is significant to note that none of these issues is absolute, which means the particular issue, concern, behavior, or belief isn't always occurring. The best way to approach this "psychological insight inventory" is to think about how you react to certain circumstances under pressure or stress or when you feel highly anxious. Anxiety tends to amplify these issues. When you feel calm, you tend not to exhibit these symptoms to the degree that has sabotaged your career.

*Shame.* The most destructive, troublesome, and least understood professional issue of the seven, shame is essentially the feelings, thoughts, and core beliefs about yourself that you are defective; not good enough; a failure; an incompetent, incapable, awful person; worthless; a phony; and damaged goods. You are fooling everyone that you are something other than these awful inner feelings. No matter what you do, it is never good enough to get rid of these feelings of shame. Given the right circumstance, these shameful feelings will flood your mind and heart within a moment's notice. All the money, promotions, professional relationships, fast cars, new houses, vacations, business ventures, sex, or compliments in the world will not erase this type of shame from a person's mind and heart.

When shame rears its ugly head, it is a paralyzing emotion that will sidetrack any adult at a moment's notice if it is not properly understood and healed. Shame is not the same as guilt. Guilt is always associated with an action or behavior. Guilt can be very productive and useful in directing a person's moral and ethical behavior. Guilt always has the capacity to be resolved and removed with an apology or corrected external behavior. Guilt can serve a positive purpose. Many times guilt is merely a behavioral gauge of a person's morality.

Shame has no functional purpose or use in one's professional or personal life. From any mental health perspective or theory, shame is useless, unnecessary, and problematic. A defective inner feeling that is not based on any type of behavior, event, reality, or action, shame is a free-floating emotion that can, at any random moment, overtake its victim. Shame can take the form of an anxiety attack when it is allowed to run wild in a person's life or of making impulsive decisions or no decision at all. Worse, shame can translate into highly irrational behavior with colleagues and clients. Shame is emotionally, mentally, psychologically, and professionally debilitating to its subjects.

We will discuss in the fathering styles section how shame is developed and carried into adulthood and the workplace. It is important to have a working understanding of what many psychologists consider an "emotional cancer." If the roots of shame are untreated, its power will continually increase in a person's life to such a point that mental, emotional, and physical health can be adversely affected. Shame has its roots in the parent-child relationship and has to be understood from its inception. Put a check next to the following questions if they apply to you in the workplace at critical, stressful moments or when you are feeling very anxious.

## Shame Checklist

\_\_\_ Do you sometimes randomly feel that you are inferior to your coworkers for no apparent reason or cause?

\_\_\_ Do you worry that you are far less capable, even incompetent, than you appear, and your coworkers surrounding you will find out?

\_\_\_ Do you fear that you are "damaged goods" and not worthy of an excellent job or promotion?

\_\_\_ Do you feel that you have done an excellent "acting job" up to this point in your career?

\_\_\_ Do you periodically experience extreme amounts of shame when you have been embarrassed or a possible professional or personal weakness has been exposed?

\_\_\_ Do you avoid certain career challenges, opportunities, and clients in order not to experience shameful feelings?

\_\_\_ Have you ever revealed, or discussed with anyone, your shameful feelings about yourself and career performance?

\_\_\_ Do you think your career would be different if you resolved your shameful feelings, wounds, and beliefs?

___ What is the one thing that you are most ashamed about? (This may be something that you have never had the courage to admit to yourself.)

___ Do you spend some of your workday energy making sure that no one finds out about the "real you"?

Seriously consider the questions above and their relevance to your personal and professional perception of yourself in your daily life. If you answered these questions in the affirmative, consider the possibility of how your shame-based feelings are holding back your career. This may sound "corny" or too simple, but don't allow shame to hold you back from healing it. The role of shame has to become less and less of a force in your life.

*Self-doubt.* A close cousin of the shame family, self-doubt is the nagging undercurrent in your mind that you are incapable, not incompetent, and/or unqualified for the position, the decision-making process, or a career promotion. You always have a high degree of uncertainty about every decision you make. You lack self-confidence and clarity about your role and your position in the workplace. This uncertainty is present whenever you have to make any type of decision or commitment or have to set limits with an employee or a client. Self-doubt is different from shame in that it is an emotional insecurity that is based in your job performance and role. Self-doubt is a condition that you feel uncomfortable about yourself when you have to make a definitive stand. You just aren't sure how to handle situations where you have to make decisions, say no to an employee, voice your opinion, or be the final word on a project. You don't question your role or position in the workplace like your shame-based colleague does. You just feel insecure, tentative, unsure, uncertain, and doubtful of your professional actions. You worry excessively about making the wrong decision to the point of being incapable of making necessary timely choices. Constant worries are based on the self-doubt of your abilities mentally, emotionally, and professionally. This emotional block eventually becomes the undoing of your forward career movement.

Consider the following questions about the dynamics of your self-doubt and the role it plays in your career. It is normal to have some degree of doubt. What is being described here is an excessive amount that becomes a major roadblock to your career advancement and, in the worse case, your daily functioning. Self-doubt is an anxiety that is not always present. For the purposes of clarification, recall that shame is an emotional condition that is almost always present and functioning. Self-doubt is difficult to understand because it creates an illusion of "business as usual" to avoid these anxious feelings of self-doubt.

## Self-Doubt Checklist

\_\_\_\_ Do you second-guess and constantly question a business decision?

\_\_\_\_ Do you generally agonize over making a decision?

\_\_\_\_ In order to keep your self-doubt anxiety low, do you become a "people pleaser"?

\_\_\_\_ Do you avoid making decisions or choices or having to say no to a client, employee, or supervisor?

\_\_\_\_ Do you sometimes avoid an uncomfortable situation by not voicing your opinion or thoughts?

\_\_\_\_ Do you say yes so that no one in the workplace will question you or your position on a matter?

\_\_\_\_ When you doubt yourself, will you go back and change your decision to lower your anxiety, regardless of the consequences?

\_\_\_\_ Do you ignore your common sense, your personal insight, and your professional experience when making a decision?

\_\_\_\_ Will you deliberately avoid a work situation, client, or personnel issue to keep from feeling any degree of self-doubt?

\_\_\_\_ Do you wonder what your career would be like without your self-doubt operating at critical times?

If you answered a number of these questions in the affirmative, or if these questions seemed close to how you feel in the workplace, consider the role that self-doubt plays in your career.

*Lack of focus.* This is a result of the two issues noted above in the workplace operating in your life. It is very difficult to focus on your career when you are full of anxiety (self-doubt) or are subject to shame or any type of debilitating emotion (depression, fear of change, panic). A lack of focus is generally the result of other emotional issues that aren't resolved or properly understood in your life. The symptom is the inability to concentrate or stay focused on a task, project, or business plan. Focusing isn't the problem; it is something below the surface in your life that is keeping you from being able to stay in the moment. Your inattention could be the result of mental or psychological concerns or problems. There could be a fear of abandonment lurking in the background that constantly keeps you from putting down roots in your current career. You could be suffering from an emotional loss that is being replayed in the workplace or with your clients.

Lack of focus can many times be a gauge for the need for a change. Many professionals will fall into a rut and become bored, uninterested, and too comfortable to make necessary changes. These types of feelings and thoughts should be considered a warning sign that a career transformation is necessary. Consider your inability to focus on a task as purely a source of information. Your behavior is telling you something. The inattention is always about a lack of interest or concern or about being overwhelmed. This behavior is not a symptom of the popular diagnosis of adult attention deficit disorder, which is more a medical problem and is generally treated with medication. Instead, a lack of focus means having problems returning phone calls at work, sitting at your desk, following up on clients, and following through on projects. There is a missing gap, step, or misfiring in how you are getting tasks, work, and projects done at work. Your work behavior is troubling to you because you know that you can do more and that you have greater potential.

Consider the following questions and how your current behavior at work might be a sign for other pending issues in your professional life. Many daughters and sons have found that once they address the underlying issues, concerns, and needs in their life, their ability to focus dramatically improves. Many times the lack of concentration is a recent onset that has gradually worsened over the months or last two or three years. Focusing isn't an issue that plagues most adults. Rather, it appears at critical times in your life, alerting you to a problem.

## Lack of Focus Checklist

___ Have you begun to notice your inability to focus on things at work?
___ Have you ignored some of your thoughts and desires in the last few months and years?
___ Do you daydream about having a different job, position, and career? What would that job be and how would it look?
___ Do you feel trapped in your current position or career?
___ Has your lack of focus been of concern to your supervisors, clients, and colleagues?
___ Do you find ways to avoid your work?

___ Do you have a difficult time more days than not getting to work in a timely manner?

___ Do you create ways to avoid working and taking on more professional responsibilities?

___ Are there things at work that excite you and grab your attention?

___ Do you believe that "focusing" could reshape your career and life?

___ Do you feel that you can have a career that fully engages you?

___ What are the emotional issues that bother you in your personal life?

Consider how you can begin to focus on the things that are important to you and career development. The above questions are designed to help you address some of the underlying issues that distract you from the kind of career and fulfillment that you desire. Concentrating is often related to how we feel about our self, our career, and our potential. The clues for your lack of focus can be traced back to anxiety, which maybe very subtle at times. Resolving your anxiety and understanding your dad's style of fathering are the keys to regaining your career focus and drive.

*Motivation.* If there is one common word more than any other that is used to describe a prime employee, "motivated" is the one. Careers are made and lost over the perception of one's motivation at work. The actual word *motivation* means drive, incentive, a need or desire that causes a person to act. The reason people go to work every day, choose a particular career, make certain decisions, and behave a certain way are all gauged by their inner motivation. When a person has a clear desire for something, whether it is a new position or a long-term goal, it is fueled by motivation.

Plenty of research has been done on the dynamics of motivation, and it all comes down to what you desire becoming your driving force. There are many areas of a person's life (personal, professional, relational, and financial), each having its own set of motivations, wants, and desires. It is important to know what drives you on a daily, and even on a yearly, basis for the purpose of being empowered. Once you're empowered with this knowledge, then you can accomplish what you desire.

According to the famous research psychologist Carl Rogers, certain needs have to be met in an individual's life in order to reach higher-level motivations such as professional success, financial stability, and inner personal and career fulfillment. The problem for many professionals is that their motivation has been lost or no longer focused in the right direction for their career, draining a person's career momentum. Though lack of motivation and lack of focus are very similar, they are also very different. These two career roadblocks need to be separated in this discussion so that their critical importance can be better understood from the perspective of the father factor. You can be motivated but still have a lack of focus toward your goals. It is very difficult to be focused without a clear motive and direction.

Whether you have a small family business or work in a large corporation or at home, people with motivation almost always do well. This discussion isn't a moral judgment on what types of motivation are right, wrong, good, or evil. It is assumed that any sincere discussion of motivation is from the perspective of enriching a person's life and benefiting the people surrounding that life. Many professionals will experience significant life changes outside the workplace, including getting married or having and actively raising children. These important life changes require a realignment of one's motivation and career objectives. It is wise to update and reexamine your motivation in the workplace based on all the different variables in your life. Your career and personal motivation will be different at age forty-five from what it was when you were thirty. The same holds true for a twenty-eight-year-old versus a fifty-four-year-old professional.

If you find yourself lacking motivation in your career, consider the following questions to help refocus you on the process.

## Motivation Checklist

\_\_\_\_ Do you know what motivates you at work today?

\_\_\_\_ What three things are currently very important to you in your career?

\_\_\_\_ Do you have a plan for accomplishing your professional one-, three-, and five-year goals?

\_\_\_\_ Are you aware of your innermost desire in your career?

\_\_\_\_ Is there a motivational role model for you in your career?

\_\_\_\_ Do you dread going to work more days than not?

\_\_\_\_ How much effort do you put into your career today versus five years ago?

\_\_\_\_ Would you consider yourself as motivated as your professional peer group colleagues?

\_\_\_\_ Would your colleagues, supervisors, and clients consider you a motivated professional?

\_\_\_\_ Do you desire to change careers?

___ Do you have a career passion?
___ Do motivation, professional drive, and focus play a role in your day-to-day work life?

These questions are designed to raise the issue of your motivational concerns and drive at work and in your personal life. It is impossible to be motivated in one area in your life and not have it spread to other areas. Motivation can be the jet fuel in your career gas tank or the lack of it—a ball and chain preventing you from moving forward. The disappearance of motivation from a career is subtle, and no one is immune to its occurrence. Maintaining high levels of motivation can come from insight derived from understanding your father's influence on you.

*Personal responsibility.* This is one of the strongest father factor influences in a person's life. The ability to take personal responsibility for your career sidesteps many of the common emotional pitfalls and mental roadblocks that hinder a person's career development. For example, personal responsibility in your career is not about blaming your father, finger-pointing at others for a failed promotion, or avoiding your personal involvement in a difficult work situation. Rather, it is examining and understanding your role in any given situation, good or bad. A person who doesn't blame others in the workplace is a very powerful force. Personal responsibility breeds ethical behavior, ethical thinking, and creative problem solving and foresight for any type of decision or action. Your emotional and mental energy isn't wasted on defending your actions or position or trying to convince people of your innocence in a given situation.

It is impossible to have any degree of professional integrity without the understanding and practice of personal responsibility. No significant career advancement will occur unless these inner qualities and understandings are in place in a person's life. The corporate scandals of the last few years are painful reminders of what happens when people in the workplace think that their actions occur in a vacuum. Those same people cause tremendous suffering to millions of others as well because they don't feel personally responsible for their thinking and actions.

Professional insecurity, low self-esteem, shame, a lack of focus, and self-doubt all factor into the inability to take full responsibility for your actions. Becoming more responsible for your actions is one of the ways to lower your career anxiety and stress and garner immediate respect in the workplace. It is the absence of personal responsibility that is the underestimated problem behind most stalled careers. Becoming responsible for all your career choices can be very overwhelming and quite liberating at the same time. The understanding of this puts your career development right back in your hands. *Personal responsibility breeds personal power.*

When adults accept that there is no one to blame for what's not happening in their careers, that creates personal empowerment. How many times have we heard people describe their work situation in such a manner that they had nothing to do with their termination or their sense of fulfillment? It is always someone else's fault or outside of his or her control. These types of beliefs are rarely, if ever, accurate and are very naive rationales for adults. Understanding where you stop and start in a given circumstance, in a business deal, or in a project allows you and your colleagues to function at their potential. It is the sign of high-functioning adults when they don't think twice about being responsible for their actions and choices.

If the following questions raise some concerns about your ability to be personally responsible for your actions, consider how to change that pattern. It is never too late to begin to be the type of person who is responsible for his or her career and all the decisions that go along with that action.

## Personal Responsibility Checklist

____ When a problem arises at work, do you automatically become defensive and argue that it is someone else's fault?

____ Do you blame or pass on responsibility for a problem or missed opportunity in business?

____ Is it difficult for you to receive critical feedback about your performance?

____ Do you consider yourself the type of person who takes personal responsibility in all areas of your life?

____ When a client is right about a problem and you're wrong, will you acknowledge it or try to make up excuses for it?

____ Do blame and resentment have a role in your career?

____ Do you "talk" someone down to a supervisor or colleague to better your position?

____ Do you consider yourself ethical in your career?

____ Did your father take much personal responsibility for his career choices?

___ Do you think or know if your father was ethical in his career and his business dealings?

___ Do you deliberately twist the truth in order to better present your position or product?

___ What role does personal responsibility have in your daily career performance and your future career development?

These questions are very important to ponder if you are going to move past career roadblocks and to maximize your knowledge of the father factor. Your ability to be responsible for your actions and decisions is the road to gaining the things that you desire in your career and, more important, in your life.

*Emotional immaturity.* This may sound out of place, but it is as critical an element in the workplace as anything discussed so far. It might be easier to describe an emotionally mature person and her responses in the workplace than the opposite: the ability to handle without reacting and to process and understand someone's emotions, position, and thoughts. You have the ability to see another's perspective, belief system, and opinion separate from your own perspective. You don't project your feelings and thoughts onto others. You don't assume that everyone thinks and reacts the same way as you do to a stressful situation. In order for you to feel good about yourself on a personal issue, you don't need for everyone to agree with you.

Second, emotional maturity is the ability to process, understand, and express your own thoughts, feelings, and needs in a constructive manner. Emotional immaturity is the inability to express your feelings and understand them without projecting them on to everyone else in the workplace. Chronic anger is a sign of emotional immaturity. It is the inability to rationally understand another's perspective and express your frustration about a particular situation. Anger is not a problem unless it is the only way to communicate your thoughts and feelings.

Another element of emotional immaturity is a low frustration tolerance. People who suffer from a low frustration tolerance have what is commonly referred to as a "short fuse" for anything that doesn't go according to their expectations. Low frustration tolerance impairs your ability to see things from a larger perspective. Developing a higher frustration tolerance allows a person to become patient and understanding rather than to be seen as a hothead in the workplace. All addictive behaviors are driven by the emotional inability to tolerate any degree of frustration or distress. In order to get away from these uncomfortable feelings, they use and abuse mind-alerting drugs or legal or illegal substances (e.g., alcohol or marijuana or prescription pain relievers). The goal of all excessive drug use is to numb the feelings of frustration, hopelessness, and emotional pain. The emotional maturity level of most addictive behaviors is fifteen years old. This emotional block keeps a person locked into adolescent thinking and over, reacting to life's challenges. The workplace thus becomes a continual source of frustration. People who are emotionally immature will try to avoid any work situation that is challenging and potentially frustrating. They simply can't handle or process the ups and downs of life, work, and relationships.

Clear thinking and remaining calm reflect the personal belief that the world's a safe place, which allows a person to develop the emotional stamina to withstand the unpredictability of work, clients, and supervisors. Uncertainty, risk, and speculation are all elements of the father factor and relate to one's emotional maturity. Consider your ability to handle stress, anxiety, disappointment, and frustration at work through the questions below. Your emotional maturity is critical to your ability to move forward in your career and in your life. All these issues are related to how your father factor operates in your daily life.

## Emotional Immaturity Checklist

___ Do you have a difficult time expressing your frustration to coworkers?

___ Do you have a tendency to blow up quickly over seemingly minor infractions at work?

___ Have you ever been told by a coworker, supervisor, or client that you are an "angry person" or a "hothead"?

___ Do you know if people are scared, reluctant, or hesitant to confront you about situations at work because of your response?

___ Do you often worry about how you emotionally handle stressful situations in your career?

___ Do you have a difficult time emotionally and mentally with changes in the workplace?

___ Do you consider yourself a person with low frustration tolerance for things in the workplace?

___ How do you emotionally handle disappointment at work?

___ Have you ever been so anxious about a situation at work that you either quit your job or had to take a leave of absence?

___ Do you consider yourself an emotionally mature person in the work-place? If so, how do you handle conflict?

___ What is your greatest source of frustration at work currently? How are you handling this situation in a productive manner?

Consider these as inquiries into your psychological and emotional state of health and happiness. Everyone has frustrations, disappointments, and let-downs. The key is how are you coping with these seemingly endless situations. Your career hinges on your reactions and emotional responses to these occurrences at work. The secret to emotional maturity starts with under-standing your relationship with your father and how that interaction set the emotional platform for your current career status.

*Fear of failure.* Of the six issues discussed so far, this is the catch-all basket. Most professionals will openly admit that they have had critical moments of fearing failure and have either acted on it or ignored it and acted anyway. Everyone understands the fear of failing, but very few will openly and honestly deal with it. The professionals who develop a perspective of how failure can benefit their career are the ones who gain the greatest degree of fulfillment and the highest level of personal satisfaction.

It is very important to remember that *failure* is a relative term—there is really no true guideline or standard for professional or personal failure. For instance, one woman's success could very easily be another woman's failure. The fear of failure has to be understood in a historical perspective for every individual. The messages about success and failure are central to issues of the father factor. Every father-daughter and father-son relationship had a par-ticular understanding of what failure is and isn't. Your professional motiva-tion, risk-taking behavior, career choices, and emotional health all come into play with your fear factor in the workplace.

What you learned about failing and succeeding in life started with you and your father. It is very important to understand and decode those mes-sages in reflecting on how you view your life as a winner or loser. Men and women who feel paralyzed by their fear of failure are, unfortunately, dealing only with the symptom of their problem. Fear of failing is a sign of a deeper undiagnosed issue such as depression, anxiety, shame, abandonment, and loss of love. Failing is clearly a personal issue that only you can understand about yourself. The mistake that people make is to judge their career devel-opment against someone else's progress. The rules, beliefs, and goals of succeeding are exclusively personal. Second, these beliefs are all issues that you learned growing up with or without your father. The majority of these beliefs are unconscious, which means that they end up playing out in the workplace. The more you consciously know about these issues of failing and succeeding, the more choices and power you will have over your career.

The more you acknowledge that the fear of failing, taking business risks, and following your dreams all started with your relationship with your father, the closer you will be to career and personal freedom. It is imperative that you begin to see these types of fear-factor roadblocks as issues that can be resolved and moved out of your road to career fulfillment. It is a tragedy when a man or woman allows these learned feelings of fear to rule their career. Again, remember that fear is a relative term, and it can be understood only in the context of your relationship with your father. The following questions are about the things you learned about fear, failure, and success from watching, listening, and knowing your father. Don't underestimate the power of these observations on your present-day career challenges. Even if you never knew your father or never had any relationship with him, you still learned valuable things about him via the family myths surrounding him. Your mother, relatives, and family friends all knew your father, and they transferred information about him to you.

## Fear of Failure Checklist

\_\_\_\_ What was your father's opinion, spoken or unspoken, about people who try something and things don't turn out as they expected?

\_\_\_\_ Did you ever know about a risk that your father took either personally or professionally?

\_\_\_\_ What did you learn about failure and success from your father?

\_\_\_\_ What are the father factor rules about success and failure in your family?

\_\_\_\_ Is much of your sense of self connected to succeeding in your career?

\_\_\_\_ What role does money play in your sense of succeeding and failing as a professional?

\_\_\_\_ How did your father handle failure?

\_\_\_\_ How did your father handle success?

\_\_\_\_ What is the one thing that you're the most fearful or concerned about in your career?

\_\_\_\_ What is your definition of success and failure?

___ How do you handle your fear of failure?
___ How do you handle your fear of success personally and professionally?
___ What is one thing you have done that felt successful?

Think about these questions because the answers will dictate many of the unconscious career decisions that you have made in the past. The more you understand your father's perspective on work, success, failure, and risk-taking behavior in business, the easier it is to start making the choices that will move you ahead in your career. These questions strike at the heart of the dynamic of father factor. How you were fathered is one phase; another phase is what you learned from him about your career and how to navigate the complex maze of the working world. We are working from the periphery to the center of your internalized father factor. The fear of failure is one of the strongest ball and chains around most peoples' ankles at a critical moment. The key, so to speak, is to unlock the chain, and that requires looking squarely at the issues of failure and success.

## SUMMARY

Think about and consider which of the seven father factor issues are currently operating in your career. Don't be discouraged or disheartened because you realize you've shown some nonproductive patterns of behavior in your career. The goal of this chapter was to introduce you to some of your hidden issues, concerns, and problems. Many of the above issues have a long history with you and must be diagnosed and addressed. The only way significant change can occur in your career is to fully and completely understand, to the best of your ability, the career impediments that you have struggled with at one time or another in your career path.

In the next five chapters, section 2 of the book, we are going to discuss the particular fathering style with which you were raised. Each style is relevant to the other and will begin to explain how the big seven father factor issues first developed in your life. In the third section of the book, we are going to focus on prescriptive ideas of how to address, correct, change, and help you gain the power over the career that you desire. The more you know about your own father factor, the more it can work as a positive influence in your career and life.

# Section II

# FATHERING STYLES OF THE FATHER FACTOR

Chapter 4

# SUPER SON AND SUPER DAUGHTER
## The Superachieving Fathering Style

I have always been a go-getter and have never felt really successful or like I have done enough. My dad was and still is so critical of everything I have ever done. Unfortunately, I tend to be the same way with my employees and family. Nothing is ever good enough.

—Joel, age twenty-nine

I have been accused of being a female 'Terminator' for years. I have a male approach to business, even though I am really a girly girl. My blunt attitude about work hasn't always helped me. People expect me to be sensitive and compassionate. Those types of nurturing qualities are for other managers.

—Dorothy, age thirty-two

## INTRODUCTION TO FATHERING STYLES

The next five chapters are going to describe in detail the most common styles of fathering that children typically experience while growing up. Each fathering style, while separate and individual, may overlap with the other four. You might, in fact, find that your father had a combination of several different styles, which is not uncommon. These five styles, each with its own distinctive traits, behavioral patterns, rules, and approaches to life, become over time the core substance of your father factor in your career, personal life, and the world at large. For instance, the career you pick and how well you fare in it are both directly tied to your father factor. Regardless of the circumstances surrounding you and your father (e.g., divorce, death, harmony, remarriage, abuse), you and your father's early-relationship building blocks have created the foundation on which you have built your career. Besides your career, your romantic life is often influenced by your father factor relationship, since men and women often pick romantic partners who have traits similar to those of their fathers. As you read through this section, you will begin to see the interconnections, hidden emotional ties, behavioral patterns, career roadblocks, and career stepping stones that all lead back to your relationship with your father.

Study each style closely. You will start to see the timeless connections between you and your father. The forgotten memories, hidden emotional connections, significant attachments, and keys to unlocking your career potential are all there with your father. In this section, it might be difficult to recall certain events, feelings, and thoughts about your father. But it will be well worth the effort to remember them, since your father factor holds so many of the answers about the nagging questions of why certain things happen or don't happen in your career. As you read about each style of fathering, you will also note that each one can have a positive influence on your career.

The challenging work will be to recognize how each of these fathering styles can also create certain roadblocks in your career. At the end of each chapter and in section 3, we will discuss the use of proactive tools and offer suggestions on how to avoid and transcend these predictable and often frustrating roadblocks. The fallout from not understanding our dads' fathering style is that we are left with only half the information about how to go forward in our personal lives and our careers. We need this valuable piece of information if we are going to successfully navigate the terrain of adulthood and our careers without creating more unnecessary emotional pain, frustration, and needless suffering.

I have found that nothing more quickly silences a conversation than men and women talking about how their fathers raised them. Regardless of the professional status of a man or woman, the topic of our fathers is a field leveler. No one is neutral or without an opinion about his or her father. One woman at one of my seminars told me, "My father was tough and left me with such a negative feeling about men that I have never overcome his influence." I asked this woman what kind of father she had, and she replied without pause, "My dad was a superachiever, type A, and never accepted anything less than perfection from me; I work hard, and now I am kind of like the old bastard." This woman left me speechless because she was the program coordinator and so seemingly mild mannered. Her reaction to the fathering-styles discussion exposed her unfinished business and unresolved feelings about her father in both her professional and private worlds.

## SUPERACHIEVING FATHERING STYLE— APPEARANCE AND SUCCESS

The two fathering qualities of appearance and achievement are the bedrock of this style of fathering, often referred to as the "superachiever." The style of relating and its motivation are based on the driving force of appearance, achievement, and success, but the real underlying emotional tone is one of a lack of self-worth. Children who are raised in this type of household are taught and shown the immense importance of always looking good, of being image conscious, and of winning. There are many examples of this type of father in the media.

In the Pat Conroy novel *The Great Santini,* a father is emotionally incapable of accepting that his son will surpass him physically, mentally, and intellectually. The son has always been given the constant verbal message to excel and achieve at all costs, or he's *nothing.* The problem is the conflicting but equally powerful nonverbal message "But don't be better than me." This conflict becomes the fuel for an ongoing power struggle between this father and his child. The result of this fathering style is that the son's spirit is broken, and his career development is negatively impacted. If Conroy were ever to write a sequel, it would be about how this son or daughter became the kind of professional who has constant battles in the workplace with authority figures, colleagues, and anyone who challenges him or her.

The significance of appearance cannot be minimized for a daughter or son of this type of fathering style, for appearance and achievement are everything. The superachieving father will see and respond emotionally only to his daughter's above-average standardized test scores in the third grade. The father's overemphasis on winning during the first ten years of a child's life begins to adversely affect her developing sense of accomplishment and her need to explore the expanding world. A father's need to look good by way of accomplishment, and to have control over his child, leaves a strong imprint upon his child's formative self-image. When a child recognizes that her father's value system places top priority on appearance (looking good in the eyes of the world) and accomplishment, it soon becomes the guiding force in her life. This child begins to place more importance on what others may think of her rather than on what she may think or feel. To shift the perspective to the importance of inner rather than outer qualities (honesty, love, hope, compassion, empathy) is difficult at any age.

For example, on the evening of her high school senior prom, Maggie comes out of her bedroom in a cloud of perfume, her hair swept up, wearing a form-fitting backless black designer dress. Her father, Stan, looks at her with a worried expression and blurts out, "Oh, sweetheart, that dress makes you look fat, and I don't want you to look that way." Maggie is shaken to her core by her father's insensitive comment. How can this young girl feel good about herself when her father is so painfully displeased with her appearance? Fast-forward twenty-five years—how does Maggie handle any type of professional feedback that implies that her work performance is less than exceptional? Maggie has learned from childhood that her net worth as a person is the total of her appearance and work accomplishments.

If your own father emphasized physical attractiveness, achievement, and always acting in a way that looks good, you got the message that what you look like on the outside is much more important than what you feel on the inside. You might have begun to develop the emotional pattern of ignoring your inner feelings and thoughts, especially when they conflicted with the imperative to be attractive. This way of relating to yourself becomes the template for future interactions in the workplace. The constant reinforcement by your father's actions, comments, and feelings about his expectations that you look good at whatever you do will become part of your father factor in your career development.

This style of fathering emphasizes for daughters and sons that the opinions of others are far more important than their own. It is a subtle process because achievement or lack thereof is always the outside wrapping for people to see and to approve or disapprove of. As adults, children of superachievers feel a deep sense of insecurity of who they are and what they can do. Their inner person—what they feel, think, want—wasn't nurtured and many times feels very lost in the adult career world. Unfortunately, you and your father probably had many heated fights and disagreements about what the neighbors will think about your behavior, actions, grades, achievements, career, or appearance. The so-called neighbors or your father's peer group had a tremendous impact on how you were supposed to live and look. These types of conflict can start at an early age and can persist well into adulthood and the workplace.

The innocent struggles of what a three-year-old should wear to the park, how your hair looks, what college you're attending, what career you have, your most recent promotion, and so on are all the father factor elements of the superachiever father. It is important to mention that this father has a great deal psychologically at stake in maintaining the right appearance and achievement level for himself and his children. His efforts are all designed to stave off his own emotional pain that he wasn't good enough, and thus to keep his own sense of shame in control. If everything looks great and outward success and achievement are all in the right perspective, then he can find a reprieve from his own unresolved father factor conflict.

## THE APPEARANCE-ACHIEVEMENT TEST— TWENTY-ONE QUESTIONS

The appearance-achievement test is listed below to help you better understand your father factor. This is a simple self-examination into how much emphasis you currently place on appearance and achievement in your career and life. Answer the questions with the first thought that comes to your mind; try not to edit an answer. There are no wrong answers. Only insight can be gained from this exam, and that is its sole purpose. This inventory is designed to help you see how much of a role appearance-achievement versus substance plays in your personal life, career functioning, and relationships.

- Do you frequently worry about what your coworkers think of you?
- How much of an impact to your emotional stability are your coworkers', clients', and colleagues' opinions of you (do their opinions ruin or make your day)?
- Does your worry cause you to spend large amounts of emotional energy and time on what others think of you?
- Do you sometimes find yourself thinking first about what other people think of you rather than what you think of yourself?
- How much time and energy do you spend on your appearance (some, moderate, lots) prior to leaving for work in the morning?

- What was the predominant message from your father to you about the importance of always looking good?
- What role did the theme of appearance and achievement have in your childhood?
- How did you get your father's attention when you were a teenager?
- How do you get someone's attention in the workplace now?
- What do you question first in a given situation: the perception of appearance or your inner feelings and thoughts on the particular matter?
- What role does the theme of achieving at all costs play in your career?
- Do you tend to view people as objects and as a means to an end?
- How important are appearance and achievement today in your career?
- What do you think the psychological impact of appearance and achievement have been in developing your career?
- Do you often feel shame about your achievement and appearance in the workplace?
- How much shame do you feel about failing and looking bad in front of others at work?
- Do you often doubt yourself concerning important issues or choices at work?
- Do you wonder at times about who you really are in spite of your perfect public persona?
- What role does the "appearance and achievement" theme have in your personal relationships and private life?
- What is the most important message you received from your father growing up about how you look to others and your family?
- What are your feelings about appearance and achievement today in your career?

Designed to illustrate to you how much or how little you've incorporated these paternal beliefs, these questions only begin to scratch the surface of the impact that always looking good has on the child of a superachiever. The second component of this fathering style, which was stressed in your developing years, is the powerful role of succeeding, accomplishing, and achieving at all costs. This attitude is supported by the constant need to look and appear a certain way regardless of the circumstances. This constant drive and internal pressure for achievement and appearance is, in essence, a cover-up for deeper unmet emotional issues. The problem with this appearance-and-achievement obsession is the sense of never being "good enough." The brutal side of this fathering style is the chronic sense that whatever you do is never "good enough" or up to the invisible standard. This becomes problematic in the workplace because the need to appear successful and competent is offset by this nagging self-doubt of never measuring up to your father's standard.

## DAD'S ACHIEVEMENT BURDEN—WHY SO HEAVY?

Your father's constant emphasis on achievement and perfection has it roots in *his* childhood. I guarantee (I am sticking my neck out here, but bear with me) that the only way your father ever received any type of nurturing, love, approval, and support from his father was through his (i.e., your grandfather's) accomplishments. It is important to realize that your grandfather—even if you may have never met him or never knew him well—had a tremendous impact on *your* childhood. Most men raised in the 1930s through the 1950s were expected to excel, achieve, and overcome the Great Depression (1929–39) and World War II (1939–45) like their fathers had.

This turbulent period taught a large group of men worldwide that the best and only way to raise healthy, high-functioning children was through high career and personal expectations. This belief isn't off base or psychologically unwise but brilliant and very useful. Other nurturing components of a son's or daughter's life, however, can't be ignored—when they are, this becomes the problem of this fathering style.

For instance, emotionally bonding with the children has traditionally been left to the mother, which, at best, was only 50 percent of young children's emotional needs being met. This fathering style creates a very lopsided relationship, since superachievers measure success only on a linear yardstick, which includes only the big three life and business concerns: *money, position, and power*. The superachiever father became the only yardstick in the business world for successfully raising children. Thus, this focus of parenting was primarily limited to the economic arena and how to get to the top of the career ladder. All other areas of a child's life were secondary in terms of importance to the father.

The fatherly expectations were primarily focused on succeeding at school and at business someday. These boys who married and had children in the 1950–70s were given this powerful life-saving message from their grandfathers and fathers, who, along with everyone else, had been trauma-tized by the Great Depression. As a result of this social and economic upheaval, the need to always be able to support themselves became the top priority for fathers in the subsequent four decades.

Fifty years later, daughters and sons are wondering why this formula for success is causing so much emotional pain, career frustration, and relationship failure. The adult children of this fathering style have hit career and personal roadblocks. *Success is much more than money, position, and power.* Complete and fulfilling success includes nurturing, emotionally connecting, secure attach-ment, communication, support, approval, and empathy. These weren't even a concern to most fathers thirty years ago but more like a luxury they couldn't afford. Today, you need to include this human component, or the same frustra-tions and roadblocks will continue to persist in your career and personal life.

It is impossible to develop naturally, to feel competent, and to feel emo-tionally safe while focusing exclusively on surface issues such as finances. The superachiever's narrow focus creates the opposite effect of success in his children. Rather than feeling strong and capable in the workplace with coworkers, they feel nagging doubt and insecurity. People are simply much more complex than their credit rating, net worth, or professional status. It is unnatural to approach your life, career, and personal relationships without the insight and understanding of the need for nurturing, approval, empathy, and mental support. These components are the fabric for expanding beyond your father's values by creating a career and personal balance, which will evolve into a sense of personal fulfillment.

The introduction of the balance of the emotional side of life allows chil-dren of superachievers to excel and become who they have always wanted to be. Your father's legacy and his motivation were to raise functional chil-dren. Now, in your career, you are going to take his fathering style to the next level of functioning and healing. Your grandfather and father were raised when stability and safety were not taken for granted. In light of a changing world and increased pressures at home (two working parents; child raising; juggling career, family, and relationships), the whole person has to be under-stood. There is no longer any room for just a cognitive approach to life to the exclusion of emotional and psychological sides. No career, regardless of the type, can thrive without the understanding and appreciation of the empathic and emotional side of a person. The nonhuman approach to business and relationships is an outdated one.

# BALANCING THE SCALE OF ACHIEVING-APPEARANCE

Daughters and sons growing up with the superachiever may have felt some degree of nurturing as a result of looking, achieving, and carrying themselves in accordance with their fathers' wishes and demands. But these same adult children are missing a sense of inner security, safety, and self-acceptance. Many times, these professionals sense a "hole" or emptiness in their heart and feel continually insecure about their place in the career world.

Regardless of how things have always looked outwardly for you, there is now a cumulative need for support, approval, and empathy for your inner feelings and deepest secrets and wishes. Your father factor hinges on your ability to understand this empathic component. Many adult children tend to go one of two ways in their careers and lives. The first is they take their fathers' advice and go beyond his dreams and wishes. But even then the much-needed approval from the fathers is still missing because . . . to some extent, they have become their fathers. Unfortunately, the world doesn't welcome this business behavior with open arms. In fact, rejection of others and militant approach to business and people has cost superachiever adult children unknown opportunities.

The second approach is a complete rejection of your father's values (though you are responding to them). Instead, you are a difficult employee, coworker, or supervisor. Your deliberate and defiant underachieving behavior and negative attitude is a major roadblock to your career, not your father's. Your rebellion against your father has not stopped since your child-hood. This inner father-child power struggle constantly plagues you profes-sionally. You are stuck in a civil war with your father regardless of your age, and your career reflects this internal tension. Conflict with authority, insub-ordination, and resentment are some of the different types of behaviors exhibited by this son or daughter in the workplace.

As all children mature, they may not fully realize that they have been looking to their business or personal partner, supervisor, or any other authority figure in the workplace, male or female, for approval. For you, when the approval didn't come or, worse, you were overlooked or not noticed, you may have felt a sense of shame flooding you. This chronic need for accept-ance and approval comes from years of internal neglect as a result of having or not having the "proper" appearance and of always achieving or rebelling. Adults then have an inner sense of feeling "flawed" or that something about them is wrong and damaged. Your career seems to reinforce your inner fears by how certain things, events, and opportunities have gone the other way. The lack of nurturing and emotional support from your father has created a large doubt in your mind about your abilities, talents, and career goals.

It is very difficult to move forward when you don't think, feel, or believe that you are capable and worthy of succeeding, even though on the surface you may know the right formula for success. You may have had it—the importance of succeeding—drilled into your head and heart since birth. You know all about the big three business factors: money, power, and position. Yet, at the same time, you don't really know the right formula for inner and personal success. The inner parts of your personality have never been developed or explored outside of appearances and achievement. You may know how to do a business spreadsheet, do a terrific PowerPoint presentation, and take your company public on the New York Stock Exchange. In spite of these incredible achievements, you still may wonder why you feel hollow inside. These powerful feelings, regardless of whether you're compliant or rebellious, all have the same root problem in common: *shame.*

Your shame is triggered in the workplace, and it is now the major side effect of your father's influence. Coworkers and subordinates might view you as a female steamroller or a male bulldozer. You have been labeled as a result of your outdated perspective on work and relationships, which you adopted from your father. People try to avoid any potential conflict with you because of your linear nonhuman response to issues and problems. No one has any idea that you carry a terrible weight of failure in your heart and feel paralyzing bouts of shame. You don't know the answer to solving your inner dilemma and wonder which way to go with this problem. You have considered switching careers, partners, and geographic locations, but, even if you have, the same recurring issues keep appearing.

This career rut and personal struggle may be the best possible situation for you. People change their lives and purpose only when the amount of pain and suffering are beyond their normal tolerance level. We are genetically wired to make big changes only when our emotional pain and suffering is beyond our control. Remember that prolonged frustration and emotional pain are two of the best and strongest motivators for change.

## Jim's Story

Jim, age forty-seven, came to see me after his wife of eighteen years moved out and filed for divorce, both in the same week. Upon first glance, Jim appeared to have no problems in the world. He was an articulate and educated professional. He considered making a big career change prior to the age of fifty. He gave me some background on his current marriage and the stress surrounding his life. Jim married Kathy but never wanted children—he felt uncomfortable with the responsibility and commitment of raising a child. Kathy wanted children and resented Jim for his reluctance. He had also changed jobs every eighteen to twenty-four months since his college graduation twenty-five years before seeing me. There was an unspoken tension in Jim's voice as he started to discuss his career and the numerous roadblocks that he had encountered. Jim disclosed that his father was a super-achiever and a very difficult man to be around. His father criticized Jim for everything he did, from finger painting in the first grade to the series of dead-end jobs he had held over the years. Jim said:

> I have done it all. I have worked as a carpenter, movie director, cook, and computer programmer for a bank. Currently, I am a yoga instructor. I have worked at twelve different jobs in the last fifteen years. I have not put much of myself into anything since the fifth grade. I got straight A's in the fifth grade. My father laughed and said no big deal; he did that all through school. I said to myself at age eleven, "Screw it; I am out of here!" and checked out. School after that was just serving time; it pissed my father off to no end, which I loved. In high school, I found two great drugs: surfing and marijuana. I have been coasting ever since the fifth grade, and now I am almost fifty years old. I know things need to change with me—I feel like a loser most of the time. My father was so tough on me growing up because he knew I was smarter than he was, and he couldn't accept that. He is now eighty-two years old, a millionaire a hundred times over, and still is on my ass. My ex-wife thinks I am a flake, but it's not that. I just don't want to become like him. It scares the shit out of me, and it is why I don't want children or a serious career.

Jim began to see me in therapy to discuss his marijuana addiction, his depression about his failed marriage, and his consistent dead-end career moves. He began to realize that he had spent a large portion of his adult life

avoiding responsibility in reaction to his father's chronic criticism and endless achievements. Jim knew that if he was ever going to have a stable career,
consistent income, and children, he had to get beyond his own negative
father factor. He began to see the value of nurturing and empathy and of
understanding his father's obsession with money and appearance. Jim began
to shift his father factor from being the classic underachiever, rebellious son
to a focused and compassionate adult. (The steps he followed are described
at the end of this chapter).

## Pam's Story

Pam was raised by a father who traveled three weeks out of four throughout her
entire childhood. Pam's father, Paul, was a hard-driving, high-achieving businessman in the South. Paul was a very nice man who believed that pleasing the
customer was the top priority. Family and personal pleasures came second. He
could never say no to a client, a supervisor, or an employee because he knew
that hard work required sacrifice. Pam, thirty-two years old, an interior
designer, had her father's work ethic, ambition, and professional drive. Pam
didn't have her father's friendly personality; she was rather cold and emotionally distant when speaking. Pam's two older siblings still lived near their father
and depended on him for financial support. Pam had always been her father's
bright spot and shining light. She said she often felt like a man in a woman's
body because of her approach to business and clients. Pam came to see me
because she was having chronic panic attacks about having to confront several
clients about money they owed her after she was terminated. Pam's entire career
had been built on pleasing people, creating a beautiful appearance, and
achieving the best at whatever she attempted. This business model worked until
she lost her three biggest clients in one month. According to Pam:

> I have lost three major clients in one month because I was too focused on
> the project, not the people involved. I was told by two of the clients that I
> was a female bulldozer when I spoke to the subcontractors doing the dif-
> ferent remodeling projects. The third client refuses to even speak with me
> because he feels I am too demanding and bossy. I am very surprised
> because I have always been all about the customer and getting the job done.
> I am not married, and I have given my career a 110 percent effort. My
> father's model for hard work has been mine, and it feels empty right now.
> All I do is work, return phone calls, and sleep. I have no social life because

there is no time for it. Now, I have lost 60 percent of my income for the year with these three clients choosing to finish their interior remodels with other designers. I am crushed. I have never had this type of business failure in my career until now. I have lost smaller projects before but never to this degree of monetary loss. I don't know what has gone wrong, other than these families no longer like my work and approach to their houses.

Pam in therapy began to realize that her father factor was out of balance and created major career roadblocks. Pam had never considered the human, compassionate, and emotional side of her career. Prior to this crisis, her business approach was based on getting the right designs, furniture, and construction in the house. But Pam started to value the empathic, nurturing, and emotionally supportive approach that her career had been lacking. Pam also started taking one afternoon off a week to have lunch with a nonbusiness-related girlfriend. These afternoon lunches were strictly pleasure, not a networking opportunity. Pam was shocked by her obsession with money—even though she had had numerous similar blowups before about her tough exterior, she never experienced this degree of monetary impact. She admitted that she had strictly focused her career energies on achieving a certain monetary status rather than developing emotional connections or attachments in her field with colleagues. Ironically, in focusing only on money, she lost it. This shift from being all about business to embracing the whole spectrum of emotion and friendships was a welcome relief for Pam.

## CHANGING THE SUPERACHIEVER TO A BALANCED ACHIEVER

The way out of the superachiever syndrome is to begin addressing the underlying issue of shame. Given all the things we have discussed up to this point, all the concerns about appearance, performance, and being good enough, smart enough, powerful enough, rich enough, successful enough, and accomplished enough can lead a son or daughter into the valley of despair and shame. The power of shame can be likened to a ten-lane superhighway getting washed out by a heavy rainstorm. After the storm has passed, there is no trace of the roadway. Shame in an adult's life operates much the same way; it leaves its victim without a path to follow. For many, it takes hours, days, weeks, and even months to overcome a severe bout of shame in the workplace. The residual effect is the reluctance, hesitation, fear, and trauma of experiencing it again. Over time in the workplace, people will do whatever it takes to avoid these episodes on a daily, weekly, or yearly basis. The avoidance becomes another huge hindrance in their career development. Their career choices are now governed by their shame-based behavior.

*The superachiever fathering style is the emotional foundation for developing a shame-based personality.* One of the developmental reasons for your shame was the constant emphasis on the appearance of success and achievement. Large parts of your personality, your self-esteem, and your emotional independence tend to be underdeveloped and ignored by the constant mandate to excel and look good. Now, as an executive, a midlevel manager, a self-employed consultant, a business owner, a personal assistant, or a file clerk, when you encounter a problem at the office, suddenly you are immobilized with a flood of shameful emotions ranging from feeling worthless, no good, phony, and fraudulent, to believing you are a horrible person, and you should quit your job immediately. These feelings are deeply rooted in trying to live up to the invisible standard set forth by your superachieving father many years ago. It is an impossible hill to conquer until the issue of shame is healed, understood, and actively removed.

## "WORKING" DEFINITION OF SHAME

Shame is one of the most insidious emotional issues adults will ever deal with in order to heal in their personal lives and careers. There is no quicker way to develop a more productive and functional self in the workplace than by resolving your feelings of shame and inadequacy.[1] Shame is considered by many mental health professionals (psychologists, psychiatrists, social workers, human resource personnel) the biggest emotional cancer that a person will develop in his childhood, which may last well into his adult life. The list below will help describe this nebulous problem and see its unconscious workings in your career and personal relationships. Shame is a constant negative force in a career until it is exposed and healed. It is important to note that, regardless of your perception of shame, it is always possible to heal it and move your career in a positive direction. It is never too late or too early to change nonproductive and self-defeating behaviors.

## How Shame Operates in Your Career

- You have random and excessive feelings of inferiority and guilt for no apparent reason. These feelings surface when you are stressed or worried about your public image and appearance.
- You have a private, personal belief that you are "damaged goods." No one knows this truth about you. You spend a great deal of time and energy keeping everyone from finding out about this global weakness regarding your professional abilities, intelligence, and competence.
- You believe that you are a "fraud" or "phony" to the people surrounding you or involved in your career—who may hold you in high regard. You aren't who people think you are in the workplace and in your personal life.
- You believe that you aren't capable of doing much with your career or life. This belief is contrary to the support and feedback your coworkers give you. Further, in spite of whatever you have accomplished, you still feel like a "loser"—not good enough. Nothing is good enough for your critical inner voice.
- You have a sense that, whatever you attempt, it will not work out, regardless of your abilities and effort. You struggle with depression concerning your life and its direction or purpose.
- You, deep down in your heart, feel like a "loser." Your accomplishments and success have never erased this primary childhood belief.
- You worry that your colleagues, clients, or supervisors will find out that you aren't who you present yourself to be in the workplace.
- Your peer group at work knows you aren't any "good." They are nice and respectful to you because they are professional and polite.
- Your closest friends don't know about your perceived career weaknesses or personal secrets of failure and fear. You are terrified to share your professional and personal insecurities and weaknesses with anyone, including your significant other.
- You try to keep people from knowing or ever seeing your "damaged" side in your career.
- Close relationships, whether professional or personal, scare you because you don't want anyone to know or see your "flawed" side.
- You know there isn't enough alcohol, drugs, sex, or money that can wipe the feelings of shame out of your head and heart.

These twelve elements of shame are just a sampling of the emotional terror that can be experienced in a person's life when he or she starts to feel these gut-wrenching thoughts. The key to stopping this reaction to never feeling good enough is to learn what triggers it. What are the circumstances that set this forest fire in your head and heart burning? You may feel overwhelmed by these feelings, thoughts, and images, but you must learn to recognize the consistent trigger for this shame response. Unfortunately, you have learned through repetition over the years that these feelings are part of your life and can't be resolved. That is the biggest deception that your shame behavior has taught you. You can and *must* change this response cycle in order to improve the quality of your life.

Another way to uncover this land mine in your career is to view shame as the critical inner voice that screams at certain moments. When you hear this voice in your mind, the behavioral cycle begins—for example, you have a sudden inability to make decisions, to think clearly, to keep your perspective on the issue, to handle difficult clients, to make an unpopular but necessary decision, and to confront employees or customers. Your inner sense of power, confidence, and position of responsibility is completely wiped out when these shame-based feelings, thoughts, and emotions surge and start to take control.

It is at these critical moments that a person's career will continue to move forward or will start to stall because potential career opportunities will be overlooked. Even if you function close to 100 percent efficiency most of the time in your job, you will occasionally have an unsettling experience that will trigger your shame-based behavior. It is precisely in these moments that you need to balance out your father's influence.

The way out of this maze of despair is to recognize that shame is the result of your father's neglect. You have to start to view nurturing as a healing force in response to the shame cycle in your career and personal life. No matter what your career, you will always have to deal with and relate to people. The interaction with coworkers, clients, or supervisors can trigger the shame cycle. Very few people can isolate themselves and not experience their crippling sense of shame. Don't allow your fear of exposure to drive you off your career path.

## HEALING THE LEGACY OF SHAME

Healing your shame and doubt and empowering your career starts and stops with *you*. This is the good news and one of the major premises of this book—

*you* hold the keys to your future. Remember, there are no downsides to this changing process. It's all positive! The mending of your critical inner voice, negative thoughts, outdated childhood beliefs, and feelings of worthlessness starts with acknowledging their role and influence on your career.

*This first step may sound obvious, but take a second look.* For the next two weeks, start keeping a journal of your self-critical thoughts. Write down the negative thought on one side of the paper. On the other side, write down a rebuttal to these outdated beliefs. This might seem manufactured, but it is the beginning of a cognitive shift. Nearly all your shameful feelings and actions originate in your belief system about yourself and your early father-child relationship. The most powerful and lasting way to shift your shame-based beliefs is *to change your core beliefs about yourself.* The key is to start liking and accepting yourself. Shame and the need for perfection are based in self-loathing. You need to expose these faulty core beliefs by writing them down. Once you put them on paper, they will not seem as powerful or as emotionally consuming. The rebuttal will be necessary to start a new inner dialogue with yourself.

*Second, in the workplace, people are constantly challenged to reinvent themselves so their careers can move forward.* The key is to reinvent how you think and feel about yourself. There is no more powerful force than your core feelings about yourself and your place in the world. People who update their childhood beliefs are the ones who fulfill their career aspirations and enjoy genuine success. Keeping a journal of your inner thoughts and positive rebuttals to those negative inaccuracies is mandatory. *Remember that your thoughts precede and influence your feelings.* Your beliefs precede your thoughts, so it is imperative to understand them. Very few professionals ever take time to do this internal work, but it is necessary in order to change your father's influence.

*Third, create a mantra, motto, or saying that reminds you of your new core feelings, thoughts, and actions.* This mantra can be anything, such as "I can do this"; "I am good enough"; "Everything is fine, and everything will work out in my job today"; "There is nothing wrong with me, even when I feel awful and scared." Be creative with your mantra because it will become an unconscious reminder of how you are changing your father's influence to a more balanced view of yourself. Write this mantra down and keep a copy in your wallet, purse, and car. Look at it several times a day for a few weeks. You will be surprised how quickly you can retrain your mind to stop thinking negatively.

*Fourth, consider the value of nurturing yourself.* What this means is to be more compassionate, accepting, and supportive of your abilities, gifts, and dreams. *Nurturing* tends to be a very misunderstood term. Nurturing isn't some wild concept that means you need to go to the desert and sit under a rock for years to gain some inner peace. Rather, it plays an essential role in creating new core beliefs about yourself. If you begin to believe that you can accept, like, and tolerate yourself, then you are changing the critical voices in your head. Remember that one of the missing factors in your father's superachieving style was a lack of nurturing you. Nurturing yourself allows you to find out what you like, what you really think and feel about things, and what to do with your career and life.

*How to nurture yourself.* Make a list of twenty things that you really enjoy doing, being, and/or thinking about. The list can include people, places, activities (e.g., driving, trips, working out), and events. Consider anything that gives you a sense of empowerment or that refreshes your energy and perspective. You don't have to go on a Hawaiian vacation to get to this kind of state, but consider things in your daily life. Nurturing is allowing yourself the opportunity to experience the things that make you feel good about yourself. The more things you discover that you enjoy, the more you will begin to think more kindly of yourself. No one has to like or agree that nurturing yourself is appropriate or right—this is all about knowing, understanding, and accepting those internal parts of yourself that have never been given proper attention and care.

After a period, you will begin to sense when you aren't nurturing yourself or being kind to yourself. Nurturing doesn't imply that you are self-absorbed or self-centered; it is the opposite. When you feel good about yourself, you can be more generous, understanding, and empowering to those around you in your career. People who are "self-centered" in the workplace really lack the tools to take care of their emotional and mental needs in a productive manner. Self-centeredness is a personal and professional weakness. Nurturing behavior is a strength because it is based on insight and understanding of who you are and what you need. *The nurturing aspect of your internal father factor is the road to true personal and professional success and fulfillment.* No one thrives emotionally, mentally, and physically without the active component of nurturing traits. Research has shown that newborn babies will die without experiencing some degree of nurturing on a daily basis. How are we any different as adults in the workplace? We aren't—and that is why nurturing is one of the keys to changing your father's impact into a positive force in your career.

## SUMMARY

We have examined some of the positive and negative influences of the super-achieving fathering style. Your goal is to find the balance between ambition and nurturing. The superachiever style of fathering has both strengths and weaknesses for your career development. The strength is the ability to create a game plan for achieving what you want. The goal is not to lose yourself in the process of appearing successful and accomplished. Pam and Jim in our vignettes both have learned the value of nurturing and healing the shame-based relationship that they adapted within themselves from their fathers. Having never considered their fathers' impact, they began to understand how their fathers influenced their career choices and circumstances. They have both implemented the first five steps of resolving their fathers' negative legacy and converting it into a positive force.

The five steps for changing this internalized superachieving father factor into a positive one will help you at work and in your personal life. Be patient with yourself as you begin to recognize and change your emotional and mental processes and functioning in your career and at home. The ongoing theme of change, resolution, and new self-awareness begins with recognizing and resolving your shame. The endless drive for perfection and achievement is simple but shortsighted and empty. Your life and career is a complex matter that has to be understood with your expanded knowledge of your father factor. The first step on this road begins by logging your thoughts on paper and in your mind. Uncovering your inaccurate beliefs about your defects and career limitations are huge steps toward discovering your personal treasures and untapped potential. It is important to now focus on your career possibilities, not accept or argue for your false limitations. Keep up the good work!

Chapter 5

# THE TIME-BOMB FATHERING STYLE

## Overcoming Fear and Avoidance

I grew up terrified of my father and his temper. I have always avoided conflict and any type of confrontation. My career has been stalled out with this fear of upsetting people. I have allowed some of the worst supervisors to walk over me. It is much easier to keep the peace. I hate confrontation and will always keep the peace.

—Betty Lou, age thirty-eight

I thought everyone grew up the same way I did. My father would come home drunk and angry and would get physical with me all the time. I never considered that other families weren't as violent or as scary as mine. Sometimes at work I have the same bad temper as my father. I just start yelling at people, and it is not a pretty scene.

—Michael, age twenty-nine

The time-bomb style of fathering is very problematic, yet it can simultaneously be productive for a son or daughter. The main problem is that this style is based on fear, intimidation, and emotional instability. This father expresses his anger toward his children, wife, colleagues, and the world at large without hesitation. This father is known as a "screamer/yeller" and is prone to random angry outbursts, which are unpredictable and scary for a young child constantly exposed to this chronic emotional volatility. One way that this type of father keeps order and controls his children is through sheer volume, the threat of a blowup, or some form of abuse, which could, at times, be self-inflicted, such as with alcoholism or drug abuse. In addition, he might exhibit a wide spectrum of emotional, mental, physical, spousal, and sexual abuses. While this father may sound like a runaway train wreck in Russia, he may have also created inadvertently equally powerful positive traits in his children.

Many daughters and sons of time-bomb fathers develop early in life the critical ability to read people. In order to survive their childhood and to avoid their fathers' enraged outbursts, they learned how to quickly judge moods and actions—purely a survival behavior. The emotional ability to read and successfully defuse this father can be compared to the radar system covering the Pacific naval fleet in Hawaii. The radar system is so sophisticated that it can detect any movement on the Pacific Ocean within a five-thousand-mile radius of Pearl Harbor. Because some of these children developed the same emotional radar and talent to read, understand, and address any situation at home, some often-abused children grow up to become excellent negotiators, corporate/business consultants, medical doctors, human resource people, social workers, mental health professionals, and teachers/professors. Some who emotionally survived this crazy environment have outstanding people and social skills. They also have excellent intuitive abilities concerning the issues surrounding a particular person or situation. They can sniff out unspoken tension in any work setting or personal encounter.

The unconscious underside of this fathering style is the child's constant effort to keep the peace and read the father. This peacekeeping behavior causes a child to skip many of the normal and natural developmental steps of growing up. Many of these children commonly become "parentified children." The term describes the unnatural role that a young child takes in becoming the emotional, mental, and responsible adult in the family. Parentified children don't have a typical childhood or adolescence—they don't rebel or skip school or act rudely to a teacher. These children are so obsessed and worried about being good and responsible that they don't indulge in normal developmental teenage or young adult behavior. These children have a tremendous amount of self-imposed stress about being five minutes late for school or missing one homework assignment in a semester.

The reason for this extreme psychological response is the immense fear that these children have experienced on a daily basis. When they become adults, they find it very difficult to recall with much clarity the severity of fear, panic, and terror they felt when growing up. These adults are in all levels and positions in the workplace—they avoid conflict, yelling, and expressing any degree of anger or frustration, emotional tension, or dealing with unresolved conflict in the workplace. Their career tends to be governed by the need to avoid intense emotional interpersonal situations. Yet many are highly functional in the workplace or in their own businesses. Unfortunately, these adults carry a very heavy emotional ball and chain of guilt whenever they have to say no or not please others.

## IT'S ALL ABOUT SAFETY

Keeping the peace and achieving a sense of emotional safety was the most important characteristic for children of a father with a time-bomb style. Normal mental health and proper emotional development are based on the degree of emotional safety and consistency that a child experiences as he grows up. Children learn early on that their lives are not safe when the adults are yelling for no reason, screaming at them, or hitting each other or them. Children learn that, to keep these out-of-control situations from occurring, any type of "peacekeeping" behavior is necessary.

If you were this child, making your father happy was the predominant theme of your childhood. Your life hinged on your father's mood swings and on your anger-management skills. As a result of this natural need to keep things calm with your father, you may have developed an obsession with control. This behavior is many times described by others as you acting like a "control freak." One of your problems in the workplace might be your struggle with the issues of control, trust, and avoidance. All these career behaviors have their beginnings in the overwhelming anxiety you felt as a child. As an adult, you will go to any length to avoid these terrorizing feelings.[1] Nearly all anxiety disorders have their beginnings in this style of fathering. The root problem is the emotional unpredictability of your father. This uncertainty about the future, for instance, could have been when your dad came home from work or when your grades arrived in the mail. These events helped create a constant state of terror in your mind and heart. Over a prolonged period, these fears became rooted into your mind and emotions; hence, an anxiety disorder was created. The severity of this panic response to the future is based on your experience of your father while growing up. Your anxiety may range from nearly nonexistent to extreme. Everyone is wired to have a small degree of anxiety about uncertainty, but I am not refer-ring to normal, appropriate anxiety here. The type of anxiety I am describing is all consuming and can significantly impair your daily functioning in your career. *Your anxiety, issues with control, and avoidant behavior are all related to your father's behavior.*

## WHAT A TIME-BOMB FATHER LOOKS AND ACTS LIKE: FIVE SHORT STORIES

The following scenarios might help illustrate how this type of father oper-ated at home and how he functioned in the workplace. Try to see the impact it may have had on you. Don't be surprised about the degree of denial—your inability to confront the truth about the influence your father had on your life. Remember our goal is to gain insight and understanding, which will directly empower your career potential and future choices. All these fathering expe-riences shaped your current career functioning.

*The first scenario.* Your father came home from work and immediately starting yelling at you for the mess in the front yard. His anger was so out of control that, as you walked by him, he hit you on the side of the head. You were told not to cry or you would get a worse beating. The only thing in the front yard? Your bike. Your father spent the rest of the night fighting and arguing with your mother and other siblings. You avoided your father by leaving the house or hiding in your bedroom. The next day, your father went to work early, and no one said anything about the fighting or hitting the night before. All day long at school, you worried about what might happen that night when your father returned home. No one at school knew about your inner panic about your father's mood swings and violent behavior. More severe cases of this fathering style have the added element of the use and abuse of alcohol and/or drugs (e.g., marijuana, prescription drugs, illegal stimulants), which would only amplify the danger in your home. Your home life never felt emotionally, mentally, and physically safe when your father was home. Your childhood centered around avoiding your father and his raging outbursts. This early preoccupation with fear of your father is the foundation for developing high anxiety in your adult relationships, both per-sonally and professionally.

*The second scenario.* Your father came home drunk after work. Your mother was disgusted and told him to leave the house. Your father saw you and slapped your face so hard that it knocked you to the ground. He claimed that you were being disrespectful, but you had no idea that you were doing any such thing; all you were doing was watching your parents fight. You were completely bewildered by your father's constant anger and aggressiveness. You watched your parents fight almost every night. The next day, your father had no recollection of hitting and yelling at you for an hour about how difficult his life is in supporting the family. Unfortunately, you had an excellent memory of the entire event—in fact, you remembered all these traumatic incidents each night with your father. Yet it seemed that no one else at home had any recall of these nightly dramas.

The morning after another family fight, your father took you out shopping for clothes and for a nice, peaceful lunch. You and your father discussed how things were going in school and with your friends. This complete switch in your father's behavior emotionally and mentally confused you. You knew from previous experience not to trust your father's quiet, sober side because it would be only a matter of time before the next blowup would come. No one in your family talked about your father's emotional and physical blowups or about his substance abuse. Your family's avoidance of your father's temperament and parenting style was deliberate. The only collective family goal was to keep the peace and the status quo. According to your mother, your father had a good job and behaved that way only at home. She would say that your father had a lot of pressure at work and that having a few postwork drinks allowed him to relax.

The next three scenarios are about your father's present impact on your work, home, and personal life. These are real-life work situations of sons and daughters who are struggling to change their internalized father factor. Look to see how your career might be affected by your not having realized the negative impact your father's style still has on your life.

*The third scenario is present day.* You come home from work, and the kids and your spouse are driving you crazy. You hear the kids arguing, and your spouse yelling for your help. You immediately start to yell at the kids and at your spouse because the house is messy. Earlier in the day, you blew up at the office over an insulting remark someone made to you at the executive meeting. You were so angry about the "disrespect" from your coworkers that you lost your temper at the mailroom clerk for not picking up your mail in the afternoon. Driving home, you started to feel "road rage" over the idiots on the road during rush-hour traffic. In your car, you started screaming at other drivers with the windows rolled up so that no one could hear your mental meltdown. When you walked into the house, you felt an incredible amount of tension and anger. Just like your father, you started yelling at your family. Unfortunately, your kids are scared of you, but their fear doesn't register with you, so your screaming continues. You spend the rest of the evening in front of your computer reading e-mails and doing office work, which only adds to your anger and resentment.

*The fourth scenario is also the present-day circumstances at work.* Prior to leaving work on a Friday afternoon, you are asked by your heavy-handed authoritative boss to complete a major project by Monday, which requires at least a week's worth of work. Your boss demands in a friendly tone that you take your weekend and get it done. You don't mention that you have plans with your friends to leave town for the weekend and have already paid for the hotel and airfare. Fearing your boss's angry response and disapproval, you regretfully comply and cancel your trip. Your boss is unaware of the personal sacrifice you've made to please him. You frequently find yourself in these types of situations—you don't want to disappoint anyone. Your life is always about what other colleagues, clients, and coworkers think of you, regardless of what you think or feel. You rarely will say no to anyone or to anything at work or in your personal life. Because of your inability to create clear boundaries at work, you feel underappreciated and taken advantage of by coworkers and supervisors.

*The fifth and last scenario.* This is about your temper with customers, colleagues, and supervisors. You don't mean to be condescending to or verbally critical of your staff, but you are. Your boss is constantly getting complaints about your harsh and aggressive attitude toward coworkers. You are a very hard worker and don't have much sympathy or understanding for incompetence or laziness. You had a meltdown at work today with an employee and were told to go home by your vice president because she didn't want the situation to escalate. This isn't the first time you have been professionally reprimanded for an aggressive and hostile display of emotion. In fact, you have been passed over several times for a big promotion because management is rightfully concerned about your history of verbal explosiveness with other colleagues. You explain these occurrences away as part of your modern management style. Your father factor style is like that of a good war general—mentally tough, aggressive, fearless, and willing to win at all costs. The problem with your approach is that work isn't a war zone, and no one wants to deal with you. Your company likes your excellent work ethic and productivity. Yet these frequent heated emotional encounters you've had with colleagues and clients are your career stoppers. You know you have a "hot temper" but find it hard to control under certain circumstances.

The first two types of time-bomb scenarios seemed normal and part of your everyday life in your childhood home growing up. No one questioned or thought that your father's behavior was abnormal or problematic. In fact, you think you might be crazy because you remember the nightly trauma, and no one else in your family thinks it was such a problem. Until the mid-1990s, verbal and all the different types of abuses—with the exception of sexual abuse—were considered normal fatherly business. Now, you wonder how to manage your range of feelings in a positive fashion so that you don't act like your father at home or in your business. Your inner fear is that, given the right set of circumstances, your response to stress at work might resemble your father's behavior. Your desire is to change your father's behavior into a positive influence. Yet these "flare-ups" keep happening, and your career constantly suffers.

The other three present-day scenarios are also typical reactions of children raised with a time-bomb father. Usually, either these adult children will become passive and compliant, or they will display anger, tension, and explosiveness in the workplace and at home. They struggle with anger-management issues, anxiety problems, and compulsivity issues (e.g., alcoholism or "workaholicism"). There are two typical reactions for children of this fathering style. One is completely avoiding people, becoming fearful of confrontations or of disappointing people, and eluding anything new or potentially stressful. The other is becoming more abusive, aggressive, and compulsive than the child's explosive father was. This fathering style isn't neutral or passive; no child raised in this type of environment is indifferent to the emotional trauma endured. Nonetheless, most adult children of the time-bomb fathering style prefer not to remember or discuss their childhood experiences. But, in order to effect long-term change, these childhood experiences must indeed be fully processed and understood before beginning the process of positive personal and career change.

# TIME-BOMB FACTORS IN YOUR CAREER

Adult children of time-bomb fathers appear to have certain characteristics as a result of being raised in an explosive and unstable home. The constant threat of danger (emotional, mental, physical, or sexual) or the actual experience of abuse creates certain behavioral traits in children. People who grow up in this frightening environment enter the workplace armed with their experiences and reactions. The common thread among all time-bomb reactive behaviors, beliefs, and feelings is that these children lived for years repeatedly exposed to a volatile house. It is important to note that, even if your parents were divorced and you saw your father only every other weekend, your father could still have a tremendous impact on you. Don't think that, because you didn't live with or see your father every day, his fathering style didn't influence, who, what, and where you are today. You were nonetheless exposed to a time-bomb style of fathering, which impacts your life today.[2]

The following list contains some of the more common adult behaviors in the workplace of children of a time-bomb style of fathering. Put a check mark next to each statement that describes your work behavior at times.

## Time Bomb List

___ You isolate yourself in the workplace based on a fear of people and any type of authority.

___ You are emotionally distant at work (regardless of the setting—home, office, small business, traveling) in order to avoid any type of conflict. This includes your coworkers, colleagues, clients, and supervisors.

___ You are always seeking the approval of others, regardless of your career position. This creates personal and professional identity issues for you. You must have everyone's approval.

___ You avoid any type of conflict professionally and personally. Angry people and personal criticism privately frighten you. Arguing is a very scary experience for you to be in and or to witness.

___ You have become a time bomb yourself, you married one, or both. A variation would be the attraction to another compulsive personality such as a workaholic or an alcoholic.

___ You experience strong feelings of guilt associated with standing up for your rights. It is much easier to give in to the demands of others than to voice your opinion or wishes. You have tremendous difficulty saying no to anyone, especially to an authority figure. Saying no also creates immense amounts of anxiety for you.

____ You judge yourself harshly at work and in your personal life. You suffer from a low sense of self-esteem and self-worth in your career. You have problems placing value on what you do and want in your career.

____ You have been told by numerous sources in your career close to you that you are a "rage-oholic." You dismiss these comments as misunderstandings of your style. Your partner and children all think you "yell" too much at home for no reason.

____ Your coworkers view you as fair and evenhanded or as arrogant, domineering, and difficult to work with.

____ Your style inspires coworkers, or it terrifies them.

These ten statements, about traits and common behaviors of children of a time-bomb father, are important to understand in order to begin the process of change. The issues of people pleasing, the avoidance of conflict, impulsive behaviors, low self-esteem, and excessive guilt for setting personal limits are critical to understanding and change for your career growth. No profession can carry these time-bomb features up the corporate ladder. Regardless of your employment situation, these behaviors are counterproductive to your life and well-being. The reason for change is that these issues become increasingly heavier with each year and with each personal crisis. Do any of the above statements strike a chord of recognition in your heart about your personality and behavior at work and in your personal life?

Having a time-bomb father scared you, and that fear has many ways of remaining very active in your present-day career. For instance, the horror of surviving all the different forms of abuse were very damaging to your inner picture of yourself, which can be either passive or aggressive, but ideally should be more balanced and professional. One of the goals of this book is to change that inner picture of yourself and your beliefs so that you no longer react to emotional, mental, or physical triggers from your relationship with your father. Each fathering style carries its own baggage. *This particular style carries the undiagnosed and emotional secret of anxiety.* The amount of free-floating anxiety you carry around is considerable. Whether you find yourself at work giving your personal power away or scaring your coworkers and colleagues with your anger, your behaviors are driven by hidden, untreated anxiety.

## THE BIG ANXIETY SECRET

In the first four chapters, we discussed some of the major psychological impediments that resulted from a father's behavior. These issues, left untreated, will derail one's professional growth, personal satisfaction, and career potential. In chapter 3, we discussed the seven major roadblocks to building a successful and powerful career (shame, self-doubt, a lack of focus, a lack of motivation, personal responsibility, emotional immaturity and anger, a fear of failure). Self-doubt and a lack of focus are two of those roadblocks and two psychological features of anxiety. Any discussion of anxiety has to be understood in the context of this time-bomb fathering style. Before we go any further in our discussion of anxiety and connecting the dots back to you, it is important not to minimize the terror that you as a child experienced growing up with this type of father.

Christine is a twenty-six-year-old single woman and a daughter of a time-bomb father. Christine came to see me because of her anxiety, nagging self-doubt, and lack of focus in her career and personal life. She knew some-thing was wrong and that it was time to address it. Since the seventh grade, Christine had a pattern of always pleasing people, fixing everyone else's problems, and worrying far too much about what others thought of her. Christine found herself completely overwhelmed by that year's holiday season and all the activities involved. She worked full time at least fifty hours a week as an owner/operator of a hair salon and acted as the "mother figure" to the other ten stylists. Though she was only twenty-six, Christine always derived great personal pleasure from taking care of her coworkers, her predominantly male clientele, and her group of girlfriends. But things had changed. Christine's old pattern of pleasing people wasn't working and instead caused her great personal and professional problems.

Christine had a stylist, Bill, whom she suspected was stealing from her. She confronted Bill, and he denied it. In fact, he implied that she was "sexu-ally harassing" him because he was the only man in her salon. According to Christine, "I have never had anyone accuse me of not being honest or forth-right with them. When Bill started yelling at me, I immediately felt like a little girl. I found myself wanting to apologize for even thinking he would do such a thing. Bill's insistence on his innocence immediately made me question my own thoughts and opinion. He insulted me the same way my father would always do to my mother and me. I was so upset with my lack of strength that

I didn't fire Bill. Worse yet, I told him I must have made a mistake. Fortunately, Bill quit the salon a few weeks ago. I am worried that I have no backbone when people get angry with me. When I am running late for my next client, I don't charge him if he has to wait more than ten minutes."

I asked Christine to describe her father's parenting style. Christine replied, "My father was a nightmare. He would come home from work either drunk or in a bad mood. Then, he would get into a fight with my mother. I was always scared and worried when my parents would fight. They got divorced when I was thirteen years old, and my mother fell apart emotionally. I took care her after that, and I still do. I did the housework, wrote checks, and paid the bills. None of my friends knew about how much I did at home. My mother didn't leave her bedroom for a year. I would go see my father every weekend, and he would yell at me for not caring about him. When he would get really mad, he would call me horrible names. My dad was never happy with me or with what I did. Now he is critical of how I run my business. I have always tried to help both of my parents to be happy. It never seemed to work." Christine, after describing her father's style and the emotional burden she carried for her family, started to see the connections to the present with her own style.

Over the next few months, Christine began to address her lack of focus, her self-doubt, and her inability to have her own opinion as symptoms of her underlying anxiety. She took active steps to address her father-daughter issues. The most important step she took was to begin to become consciously aware that her behavior at work was a reaction to her time-bomb father. Christine, for the first time in her life, understood that many of her activities and choices at work and in her personal life were driven by her untreated anxiety. She realized that her avoidance of conflict, always being the peacemaker, second-guessing her opinion, having low-self esteem, and needing others' approval were all connected to her father factor. Once she made the connection, Christine felt much better about her salon, her parents, and, most important, herself.

Christine's behavior is very common for a child of a time-bomb father. Many people work very hard to overcompensate for their anxiety, which has its roots in their childhood. Look at the following descriptions of anxious behavior and rate yourself and the degree of anxiety you carry in the workplace.

## ARE YOU ANXIOUS? THE CYCLE OF ANXIETY AND ANXIOUS THINKING

Anxiety is considered a normal reaction if it is aroused by a realistic danger and if it dissipates when the danger is no longer present. If the degree of anxiety is greatly *disproportionate* to the risk and severity of possible danger, and if it continues even though no objective danger exists, then the reaction is considered abnormal.[3] You can see from this description that the roots of your anxiety can be traced back to your time-bomb fathering experiences.

The following questions and descriptions are designed to show how your anxiety operates in your career and in your thoughts. Try to see how anxiety effects your professional and personal choices.

- *Minimization.* This is the thinking process by which we downplay our capabilities at work, at home, and in our personal life. We discount our personal resources, talents, and career potential. We convince ourselves that we really aren't that capable or smart enough or that we don't have the knowledge or experience to get the job done or handle the situation. Whatever the issue is, we aren't [fill in the blank] enough. The sense of inadequacy is an underlying anxiety that may keep your career on a long plateau and is very frustrating.
- *Selective abstraction.* This is the process by which we overemphasize our perceived professional weaknesses. It is normal to feel uncomfortable in new work situations. The problem is the constant avoidance of new challenges, jobs, or promotions because of a serious misconception of your abilities or talents. You put more value, energy, and power on your weaknesses than your strengths. You focus on what you can't do versus what you are capable of doing. You are much more comfortable arguing for your career limitations rather than for your career potential. This thinking process seems as natural as breathing; you don't even question the irrational reasoning.
- *Magnification.* This is "making mountains out of molehills." While selective abstraction is concentrating on your perceived weaknesses, this overemphasizes the importance and value of those weaknesses or issues. You are always worried that coworkers will view your weaknesses as personal failures or ethical flaws. For example, do you have a fear of public speaking? You likely would avoid any situation or

position that would require any type of public speaking. You would exaggerate the importance of your fear of speaking because people would think you are stupid or a poor manager. The fact that you aren't a gifted public speaker would mean your colleagues would think less of you or wouldn't respect you. The idea that you could get assistance and become a better public speaker would likely never enter your mind. You are convinced that this limitation is a career stopper for you. *The real problem is your way of thinking about it* and the inability to get past this mental and emotional block.

- *Catastrophization.* This takes magnification even one step further. It is the uncontrollable impulse to exaggerate the importance of a particular action, issue, circumstance, and/or personal conflict, then immediately imagining the most horrible outcome that could possibly take place. Every stressor becomes a "crisis" with this type of reacting. Your daily work life is a miniseries of one pending disaster after another. The ability to keep a clear perspective on an event is nonexistent. Your work and personal life are always full of impending "drama," real or imagined. This reaction style is very wearing emotionally and mentally for you and the people in your life. One of the long-range problems is that your coworkers label you as an "alarmist." After so many false alarms, you might not be taken seriously for a real impending problem because of your history of always overreacting to stress and work problems.

The following diagram might further explain the inner response cycle your father factor has in your career. The founder of cognitive behavioral therapy (CBT), Albert Ellis, developed a four-step sequence of reacting.[4] Try to see in pattern of thinking how the four issues above have become a natural response in your career. This thinking process is the problem for anxiety suffers and overreactors.

EVENT———▶THOUGHT———▶FEELING———▶BEHAVIOR

Everything we experience in life is an event. Our day starts with the event of getting up. The next step is, what do we think of that event? Unfortunately, another trait of the time-bomb father is negative thinking, which produces negative, self-defeating feelings. I once heard a poignant analogy about anxiety: *Emotions follow your thoughts like baby ducks follow their mothers.*

*That doesn't prove the mother knows where she is going.* Because we are always thinking, all of us base our feelings and behavior on what we think in response to events. This four-step thinking chain is universal and in operation every day at work. Anxious adults tend to have negative thoughts and don't usually consider the possibility or chance of another option or positive outcome. The outcome of such thinking is our behavior, which impacts our career choices, daily business decisions, and professional functioning.

The bottom line is that our anxious feelings, behavior, and reactions come from our negative thoughts, which developed in our childhood about our career potential, the world, and our place in it. In order to trace back our negative cycle of thinking and feeling, it is extremely valuable to understand the early emotional experiences we had with our father. Again, it is important to point out that all our discussions about our fathers aren't for blaming or finger pointing. Rather, the *only* worthwhile goal is to gain insight, and wisdom, so that we have the courage to change our internalized father factor in the workplace. It is very tempting to start down the road of blame, but this is a dead-end highway and very difficult to get off once it is traveled. How many people do we know who constantly blame their parents, particularly their fathers, for their failed relationships, poor career choices, and lost income?

Understanding that you can change, expand, and create new thoughts about your career, yourself, and your life is the way out of an anxious, reactive lifestyle. Adults didn't get to this place of constant negative thinking and anxiously looking at the world overnight. The angry outbursts, the substance addiction, the people pleasing, and the avoidance of conflict all have their origins in this simple anxious thinking cycle. Changing your behavior—which obviously changes the course of your career, income potential, position of responsibility, and self-worth—all starts with your thinking. The chronic exposure to a time-bomb father who wasn't supportive, approving of you, or patient created anxious defective beliefs about yourself that translated into your role in the workplace and in your personal life. *Your thoughts are the engine in your life, and your feelings are always following, not the other way around.* Sometimes our thoughts are so fast and unconscious that we don't recognize them—we only react and feel them. This is the hard work, beginning to do some thought stopping and redirection.

# THOUGHT STOPPING AND CHANGING DIRECTIONS: MARLA AND GARTH

The best way to illustrate the powerful concept of thought stopping and redirection after years of conditioning is to discuss Marla and Garth. The first story is about Marla, who was prone to time-bomb meltdowns herself on a regular basis. Garth was prone to being a "nervous" manager every day, all day long. Both of these professionals found a way to change their thought patterns and to re-create their internalized father into a positive force in their careers.

Marla is a thirty-four-year-old social worker for the county of Los Angeles, California. She graduated from UCLA and has been working for the county for over ten years. Marla is single because she doesn't want the added responsibility of a relationship, given her overwhelming job. She has reached a career plateau because of her reputation of being hotheaded with colleagues, clients, and supervisors. Recently, she received her annual performance review and was described as a female "Terminator." The reason for her female supervisor's harsh criticism is Marla's no-nonsense approach to business, clients, and coworkers. Marla has a very low frustration threshold for the problems she encounters, and she isn't considered a very warm or empathic person. Over the years, she was consistently told that she tends to be verbally aggressive, demanding, inflexible, intolerant of professional differences, and overpowering. Marla came to see me at her supervisor's suggestion.

I asked Marla about her relationship with her father, and she replied,

> My father was always mad when I was growing up. Everything was a crisis at work or a mess at home. It seemed that nothing was good enough or okay. When my Dad got upset, he was a screamer and was verbally abusive to my mother and me. Occasionally, my dad would really get mad and hit my mother. There was always tension in the house until my father died when I was sixteen years old. The damage had already been done by the time my Dad died; both of us, my mother and me, were traumatized by all the anger and abuse. Twenty years later, I can still hear my father's voice in the back of my head when I do something wrong. I really get freaked out when I hear myself yelling at clients and coworkers like my Dad did to me.

I asked Marla if she saw any connection between her current life and career circumstances and her relationship with her father, even though he died twenty years before. Marla said, "I have always wondered what kind of impact all those nightly screaming and yelling matches had on my psyche. My mother is depressed and has never recovered from my father's death and abuse. I have become aggressive like him because I am a woman in a man's world. It is tough being a woman and having men second-guess me. That is one of the reasons I am quick to be the leader at work and with my clients."

After discussing the sequence of anxiety thinking, which is constant, Marla realized the long-term effects of being raised by a time-bomb father and how it affected her career. She began to see that her own time-bomb approach wasn't effective or a positive force in her life. In fact, the pain and sense of rejection that she experienced at work with poor performance reviews was the catalyst for getting her to rethink her approach. She also came to terms with her constant anger, low frustration tolerance, self-doubt, and lack of career focus, which were the results of worrying about her circumstances far too much. Her anxiety was based on the abusive, explosive background she survived. She had never considered that many of her career responses were based on her early childhood experiences—that these shaped her career relationships and performance much more than she ever realized.

In the next few months, Marla tried a different approach that was much more cooperative, empathic, and patient with her coworkers and clients. She found that she was less anxious and much more effective and productive. Marla also discovered that some of the men that she found attractive were now interested in dating her. Her anxiety considerably lessened, and her aggressive approach to people was greatly reduced.

## Garth's Story

Garth, forty-two, is an attorney in a corporate law firm in Chicago. He has struggled since high school with paralyzing anxiety, panic attacks (symptoms include rapid heart beat, shortness of breath, loss of vision, fear of dying), social phobias (fear of interacting with people and fear of public places), excessive shyness, and chronic fear of rejection. These were always heightened by court paper deadlines, depositions to be taken, interacting with colleagues, or with opposing legal counsel.

Garth grew up as the oldest of three brothers in a small beach community in northern California. His father, David, was an aerospace engineer in the 1950–80s until he retired in 1988. David was the classic time-bomb father who disciplined his sons by yelling and by always being loud. Garth grew up fearful of his father's nightly verbal explosions with Garth's brothers, mother, and himself. According to Garth, being the oldest usually got him the worst tongue whipping from his father. What is unusual about this story is that Garth is at the opposite end of the continuum of children of time-bomb fathers. Marla is the aggressive, overpowering type, and Garth is the passive, compliant kind. These professional differences would appear to be the result of different types of fathering, but that is not the case. Marla and Garth have different reactions to the same type of fathering style of terror.

Garth is very intelligent, articulate, and an excellent writer and an even better negotiator. He has recently been passed over for partnership in the firm because of his people-pleasing qualities (avoidance of conflict, inability to say no, passivity, seeking others' approval). Garth has worked nonstop the last fifteen years to make partner. He averages twenty-five hundred to twenty-six hundred yearly billable client hours, which is more than fifty client hours every week of the year, an incredible achievement for any law practice. Garth, as a result of being passed over, began to have severe panic attacks when on the road to work with clients. While working in Los Angeles, Garth came to see me to find out and understand what was happening to him.

I asked Garth what was he so scared of since the failed partnership vote two months earlier. Garth said,

> I have worried all my life about not being successful. My whole identity has been wrapped up in this job and making partner. My father has had a good laugh about my failure and told me to never be a lawyer. My wife is also very critical of me and said I need to take assertiveness-training classes so I don't get passed over next year. This has been a horrible letdown and a big source of disappointment for me. I have worked on average six days a week to make this career promotion, and I am scared that I am not ever going to make it now. The senior managing partner in Chicago told me I missed the partnership by two votes because of my people-pleasing traits and behaviors. The two partners who voted against me didn't feel I am strong enough to handle the pressure of being partner in an international law firm. It's true, I am very nice, and that has always worked for me until now. I keep the peace at work and home and with my father.

I asked Garth if his chronic anxiety, negative feelings, and catastrophic thinking were new behaviors. He replied, "Absolutely not! I have felt this way for years, but getting the partner promotion was a way to keep these feelings under control. Now, I am scared that my colleagues, associates, clients, and partners don't respect me or think I am a capable lawyer. I feel like quitting law and becoming a full-time fly-fishing instructor in Montana. I know it sounds strange, but I am so tired of worrying about people and what they think of me and succeeding that I am burned out. My wife, since the vote, has been acting and treating me like my father did when I was a child. She thinks I am stupid and a coward for not confronting the partners who voted against me. I disagree, and I resent her and my father for their chronic criticism of me."

Over the next twelve months, Garth came to see me when he was in town on business and began to address his anxious thinking. For the first time, he started to realize that his work style was holding him back and that he needed to change it quickly. It was also the first time that he made the cognitive connection between his father's influence and his chronic anxiety. Garth became more assertive and less worried about his colleagues' opinions of him and stopped the negative cycle of thinking, which he had developed as a result of his early childhood experiences. He changed how he viewed himself, his career, and his personal world. Garth's father and wife couldn't believe his transformation and sense of personal power. At the next partnership vote, Garth was finally elected as a partner of the firm.

## SUMMARY

The first step in changing your father's impact is to become aware of the normal adult response pattern to an everyday event

EVENT———▶THOUGHT———▶FEELING———▶BEHAVIOR

as diagrammed by Albert Ellis. This simple formula for how our minds work makes or breaks our quality of life. It sounds very simple, but it is of paramount importance to understand and change your thinking cycle. The thoughts that you have when you are anxious or stressed might run by so fast that they may seem uncontrollable and unchangeable. Once you begin to recognize and reject the old negative thoughts you usually have in an uncomfortable situation, your new positive feelings (bodily or emotional) will become information and tools for change. This diagram can begin to explain why you take certain actions, reactions, or behaviors. The mystery is greatly reduced when you understand how your internal dialogue and thinking operate within this cognitive-thinking model.

Another important key is to understand your thoughts and beliefs. Write down on a piece of paper your beliefs that govern your behavior. For instance, you might believe that, if you aren't nice, people will not like you. You might also believe that you should be able to manage your career without any outside help or support. These kinds of beliefs compose the material that limits your career choices and functioning. In your journal of your personal beliefs, you might want to use the terms described earlier in this chapter—*minimization, selective abstraction, magnification,* and *catastrophization*—to help identify your method of thinking and acting professionally.

Now that you better understand your father's style, take that information and apply it to your present-day life. Your way of thinking is your ticket to changing your internalized father factor and the direction of your career. By uncovering the mechanics of your mental and emotional processes, the direction of your life is in your hands. Most people ultimately want to have that type of control and personal power. Do you? If you answer yes, keep reading. If that concept scares you, reread this chapter and see what the mental and emotional block might be.

Chapter 6

# PASSIVE WOMEN AND MEN

## Bridging the Gap

I always wondered about my father. He never seemed too excited or too sad; he just never showed any feelings. I wish he had—it would have helped me. He was consistent and stable. I long for his simple and straightforward approach to life. My dad would never understand all the demands of my family and my career today.

—David, age thirty-seven

My father always came home from work and went directly to the living room couch. He spent the entire evening there, reading the newspaper and watching TV. We all joked that Dad was either dead or he was just sleeping on the couch again. That is how I remember my father. I wish I had gotten more fathering and attention from him. I think my life would definitely be different.

—Brenda, age forty-three

The passive style of fathering is a clear break from the previous two fathering styles. This father wasn't particularly aggressive or highly outspoken about any family, career, or personal issues. The media and mainstream culture have popularized this type of father as the "1950s Ozzie Nelson, *Leave It to Beaver*, *Father Knows Best*, low-key," passive type of dad. He personified the stable, consistent, hard-working, calm, and emotionally reserved or removed father. This man would never contemplate or engage in any type of destructive behavior or abusive language toward his daughter, son, coworkers, or friends. This father tended to be an observer of life and a peripheral member of the family. The current concept of expressing your feelings would be foreign and not part of this father's worldview or style.

The passive father was emotionally distant from his children. The basic human need for emotional connection between a father and his children eventually ignited a cultural revolution for love and intimacy from the late 1960s onward. But not all fathers followed that road. The distant father caused his children to have their emotional needs met outside of this primary relationship. Children of the passive father tend to doubt their ability to communicate and to have meaningful professional and personal relationships. There are many things children of passive fathers do well—they have an excellent work ethic and stable, committed values—but the legacy of emotional distance is a critical issue to be addressed.

## WHO IS THE PASSIVE FATHER?

The passive father typically worked for the same company right after the war until his retirement forty years later. *His work ethic was based on commitment, honesty, and responsibility.* These solid core values have been adopted by you. This type of father valued his career in terms of stability and made it his top priority. Raising his children meant being an excellent financial provider to support them. The mother was the emotional broker in the family, while father funded her projects and decisions. The passive father rarely, if ever, engaged in the emotional life of the family and particularly in the nurturing parental aspects. It was an unspoken agreement in this type of family dynamic that the women did the childcare and the men did the work outside of the house. That was the standard family practice and division of labor.

The passive father never would have gone to his children's dentist appointments, attended parent-teacher conferences, or planned birthday parties. His apparent lack of involvement wasn't because of a lack of love or interest—these types of nurturing paternal behaviors just weren't part of his or his generation's perspective. Men in this era didn't pay close attention to the integral parts of the family's emotional well-being, which was clearly the mother's domain and part of her expertise. This father typified the separation of family and work—a separation that isn't much different from the separation of church and state. Each was its own realm. Your father put his energy into the boardroom, not the family room (metaphorically).

This period is commonly referred to as the "baby boom" era (from 1946 to 1964), which saw unprecedented economic growth, the expansion of the nuclear family (to 2.2 kids per household), the development of track homes in record numbers, and the global benefits of victory from World War II. In the late 1960s and early 1970s, however, there began a slow rejection of the typical roles of men and women in the workplace, at home, and in the social arena. Women and children viewed the passive father as an oppressive force and an obstacle to healthy emotional growth. These fathers had generally no idea that their behavior was causing so much emotional pain and conflict in the family. Many of these fathers were clueless that part of being a "good provider" included emotional nurturing and active physical involvement with the children. *Cautionary note:* No one is to blame for this passive fathering style, which was culturally embraced and esteemed by men and women alike. It is important to avoid finger-pointing when doing any type of historical look at our fathers and family. It does not help your progress and creates more resentment.

## THE BABY BOOMER'S FATHER—WHO IS HE?

The passive fathering style was found in more than 50 percent of all nuclear families from 1945 to 1980, according to Dr. Murray Bowen, a family research pioneer, expert, and theorist. This is a huge percentage when you consider that there are at least four other common types of fathering styles (i.e., superachiever, time bomb, absent, and compassionate-mentor) that make up the other 40 percent or so. Prior to this time in our nation's social history, fathers tended to be even *more* distant and economically strained by work (e.g., the Great Depression). The baby boom period was an incredible opportunity for men in their careers, but it also marked the advent of women finally entering into male-dominated professions (law, medicine, law enforcement, public service) across the career board. For the first time, women, albeit in small numbers, could consider a career outside of the typical female roles of schoolteacher, nurse, and social worker. This period was characterized by most professionals working longer hours, traveling more for business, staying married to one partner, and owning a single-family home. It was a very stable and straightforward approach to life, work, and parenting.

Mothers carried the emotional load for the family. Despite some progress made by a minority of women, fathers generally carried the financial load. No one questioned this order of things until many women demanded careers, and they couldn't shoulder the emotional health and development of children alone. Even as the parents of baby boomers are entering their senior years (seventy and older), their traditional roles are still their norm and family pattern. When their children were still at home, passive fathers commonly belonged to a church, synagogue, or parish and were active in the community on the weekends.

All the activities and cultural beliefs of passive fathering created the undesirable split between fathers and their children. In today's environment, Ozzie would not make Harriet happy; she would expect him to be more emotionally involved in Ricky's and David's lives. The hallmark feature of the passive father that *he showed his love through actions rather than words.* This behavioral pattern defined for an entire generation of professionals how to act and treat people in the workplace and in many homes.

The crisis for sons and daughters of passive fathers involves having incorporated the values of their fathers into their own roles as professionals, parents, and partners. It is the learned inability to express and translate their values, thoughts, and feelings into emotional language that is the legacy of the passive fathering style. This emotional block is very problematic for people of all ages in their lives and careers.

The abilities to communicate with others and to be emotionally connected to a project, one's coworkers, and a career path are necessary for any degree of success. These much-needed qualities aren't the strengths of this fathering style, however. The reoccurring pattern of being emotionally distant is a major stumbling block. The passive father never faced the emotional demands that so many professionals confront today. The challenges of several career changes and contemporary marriage and its division of household duties, as well as the need for greater emotional expression and intimacy professionally and personally, have many sons and daughters of passive fathers panicking. Their fathers' work ethics and life experiences don't seem to "cut it" or be a source of comfort. The deep despair is felt in boardrooms, offices, business meetings, and other parts of these professionals' lives. The question that looms large is, How do I emotionally connect to, communicate, and interpret others' thoughts and feelings? There are so many things that these sons and daughters gained from their fathers, but the one major pitfall is the emotional distance that defines their relationship style.

# PAT, MARK, LAURA:
# THREE GENERATIONS OF THE FATHER FACTOR

To fully understand the ramifications of being raised by a passive father, let's look at the relationships between retiree and grandfather Pat (age eighty-two); his son Mark (age fifty-six), a professional; and a recent college graduate and granddaughter Laura (age twenty-three). Pat, a classic passive type of father, has led an admirable professional and personal life. He's been happily married to the same woman for over fifty-five years. He's had an excellent, fulfilling career in the aerospace industry in satellite development and has had good relationships with all three of his children. In fact, Mark can't remember a time when his father complained about any issue in his life or became seriously angry with anyone in the family. Growing up, Mark was convinced that his father had everything figured out in life. Mark's overall life experience nevertheless is quite different from his father's, and that troubles him deeply.

Mark's professional and personal life has been more difficult than his father's ever seemed to be. An investment banker by profession, Mark was laid off recently from a company he liked. He's been struggling to emotionally deal with this career setback and the resulting financial losses ever since. On top of that, he was divorced a few years ago from Laura's mother. Although he has remarried, he is still struggling with all the typical postdivorce issues, such as spousal support and "competing" for Laura's affection and time. Mark came to counseling because he knew that he needed to make some serious changes if his career and personal life were going to move forward. Mark told me that he frequently feels like a failure and is depressed. He often compares his life with that of his father and knows he comes up short. Those father-son comparisons are very depressing and create a sense of hopelessness in him.

His daughter and ex-wife have repeatedly informed Mark that he is emotionally distant, aloof, and cold. Laura repeatedly tells her father that she would never work for him because he is a noncommunicator. These comments about his communication style aren't new information or surprising to him. In fact, prior to being laid off, Mark was advised by his business partner that coworkers felt that he wasn't friendly or particularly interested in their projects. Mark says that he is truly interested in others. It is a shame, according to him, that he doesn't communicate the positive thoughts, verbal support, and feelings of approval of others that he sincerely holds.

Mark has tried to talk to his father, Pat, about these professional and personal communication issues. But Pat does what he has always done when Mark has attempted a heart-to-heart conversation: He rubs his forehead like he has a headache and tells Mark not to worry, that everything will work out. It is this type of emotional impasse that has taught Mark not to share his feelings or thoughts about any emotionally charged issue. Once, when Mark was ten years old, he remembers being bitterly disappointed when he failed to make his Little League All-Star team. He came home in tears and rushed toward his father. Rather than comfort his son, allow him to express his disappointment, or even yell at him for being a crybaby, Pat ignored the tears and started talking about a completely different subject. This was a normal emotional response for Pat with his children, wife, and colleagues.

Mark's approach to life and business has been shaped by these types of early emotional disappointments. Mark is greatly concerned that his daughter, Laura, has the same style as her grandfather and him. Laura, when asked about this issue, is verbally aggressive toward her father and blames him for being a poor communication role model. Mark has brought Laura to therapy to discuss the paternal legacy of being a noncommunicator and being emotionally unaware of other people. They have begun to engage their thoughts and feelings about the divorce, their careers, and their relationship. They agree that the passive fathering style has many strengths (e.g., strong work ethic and stability). It is the emotional distance and lack of communication that are the difficult parts to get past.

Through his therapy, Mark has begun to change his style in his career and with his daughter. Mark is much more aware of others' feelings and the value of being empathic. Now that he has been hired, he has found that his sense of professional satisfaction has increased with his new position as a manager of a corporate mutual fund account. He had expressed in the interview process that he was developing a stronger sense of communicating and emotional empathy with his coworkers. His employer found this type of disclosure his most valuable asset. The emotional insight set him apart from the other candidates and landed him an excellent job and career jump.

Laura and Mark, for the first time in their relationship, are having weekly dinners and discussing personal and family issues. They have never discussed anything other than superficial topics and trivial matters. Laura reports that her approach to coworkers and supervisors has improved. She, too, has become aware of her emotional distance from coworkers, as well as in personal and romantic relationships. Laura has spent much of her adolescence and early twenties blaming her father for being physically distant and emotionally unavailable to her. Now that Mark is attempting to deepen his relationship with Laura, she has to resolve her own emotional reluctance and poor communication style. Mark and Laura are both changing by becoming aware of the value and importance of being emotionally engaged in their professional and personal relationships.

## CHANGING THE LEGACY—OVERCOMING NEGLECT

Children of passive fathers grow up wondering how to resolve, understand, and communicate their inner thoughts and feelings. The learned behaviors of ignoring, discounting, or avoiding emotions and feelings breed the long-term sense of neglect in our lives and careers.[1] The benchmarks of all mental and emotional health hinge on a person's ability (1) to have clarity and insight into his personal thoughts and feelings (neglect clouds a person's ability to have the kind of clarity necessary for continued career success) and (2) to express these thoughts and feelings with a high degree of passion and empathy. We discussed in chapter 5 the cognitive cycle promulgated by Albert Ellis on how we react: *events———➤thoughts———➤feelings———➤ behavior.* Part of understanding this cognitive cycle is our ability to comprehend and process both what we think and feel.

We are going to take a serious look at why is it so difficult for so many adults to overcome the legacy of the passive fathering style, which, by default, helps create two of the seven major career roadblocks—a lack of motivation and a fear of failure—which result from personal and emotional neglect.

When, as a child, you aren't engaged mentally, emotionally, or physically, you will develop a sense of neglect for your personal needs and wants. Your functioning in the workplace will have this missing piece or oversight in how you deal with your coworkers and professional development. Neglect is a very subtle psychological phenomenon to understand and to change. On the surface, your life looks fine, but there are some missing emotional pieces and an absence of positive self-thoughts. A lack of motivation and fear of failure might appear only at critical moments in your job and at promotion opportunities.

The concept of neglect can be likened to jelly. It is very hard to nail jelly to a wall. It is equally difficult to understand the dynamic of emotional neglect. Another way of understanding emotional neglect is to examine how you feel about your own needs and wants, both personally and professionally. By inspecting how much importance you give to your inner thoughts, dreams, and desires, you are beginning the process of healing the cycle of neglect in your life. Many adults would rather discuss anything other than the neglect they experienced growing up.

One of the classic examples I have ever heard about paternal emotional neglect was from my client Gina (age forty-two), who was born and raised outside of Chicago. Every Wednesday afternoon during the winter, she (from ages six to thirteen) would have ice-skating lessons. Usually, two out of four Wednesdays, she was the last child to be picked up by her father, and that was thirty to forty-five minutes after the class ended. Once a month, her father would completely forget to pick up Gina. She would call her house an hour after the class ended to remind him. Gina said that she remembers standing in the snowy dark waiting for her father to pick her up. She was embarrassed because all the other kids were always picked up immediately after the class. As an adult, Gina has a difficult time making and keeping close emotional relationships with coworkers and friends. She assumes that no one is really interested in her, her wants, and her career. She has begun to resolve her deep sense of personal and professional neglect by doing the exercises at the end of this chapter. Gina admits that many times she still feels like she's nine years old, standing outside in the dark, cold, snowy night waiting for her father.

Self-neglect naturally results from a passive fathering style. Children feel loved, care for, and supported when the adults in their life know and are engaged with them. Gina never felt loved or cared for by her father. She felt that her father looked after her basic needs but nothing much beyond that. One of the emotional issues that springs from neglect is depression, which directly affects our career motivation and sparks a fear of failure in the workplace. Neglect, many times, is another word for depression. To overcome emotional neglect, we need to address our own sense of neglect and depression. Think about the following sequence of events that are related to adult depression:

neglect———▶lack of motivation———▶fear of failure———▶depression

# RECOGNIZING DEPRESSION

Depression results from emotional neglect. Adults who suffer bouts of depression also feel neglected by the loved ones in their lives. Depression is the emotional, mental, continuous thought process of feeling unloved and uncared for; it is a sense of emotional loss. These feelings are based in a core belief that you are unworthy of having good things happen in your life and career. When a person is depressed, it is almost next to impossible for her to have the courage and hope to take on a challenging professional risk or a new job or to be occupationally creative. Depression is an energy drain on its sufferers and the people in their life. There are many degrees of depression, all of which are important to understand.

It is significant to note that people who experience a death in the family or who go through a divorce or a sudden job loss will naturally feel depressed. Those circumstances are generally time limited and different from the ongoing sense of sadness and lethargy that plagues adults with depression. Grieving is another important form of depression that is directly related to an external incident or tragic event. Our discussion here is about the type of depression that isn't directly connected to a recent external event and does not have a direct cause.

*The Diagnostic and Statistical Manual of Mental Disorders*, fourth edition (DSM-IV), is published by the America Psychiatric Association, and it portrays depression as a chronic mood disorder that occurs for most of the day, more days than not, for at least two years. Adults with a depressed mood describe their feelings as sad or "down in the dumps." During these periods, at least five of the following additional symptoms are present. Make a check mark next to each symptom that you have experienced recently:

___ poor appetite or overeating—craving comfort foods (e.g., pizza, nachos, chocolate, all types of junk food)
___ insomnia or hypersomnia
___ low energy or chronic fatigue
___ rapid mood swings—feeling great, then suddenly feeling sad; bouts of uncontrollable crying
___ low self-esteem—in spite of current career or personal success
___ poor concentration or difficulty making decisions
___ feelings of hopelessness

____ hyper self-criticism

____ self-perception of being uninteresting or incapable of functioning in the workplace

____ increased use and abuse of alcohol (binge drinking), any increase of legal or illegal drug use (e.g., painkillers, marijuana, speed, valium)

____ body image issues—irrational concerns about weight gain or weight loss

____ loss of interest in work, hobbies, friends, and family

____ avoiding close friends and family as well as colleagues and clients at work

____ fantasies of dying

____ fantasies of moving away and starting your life over alone

____ sudden change in your routine for no tangible or rational reason

____ overemphasis on work, career, and money matters to the exclusion of any other personal matters

____ people close to you have noticed your mood change (e.g., significant other, colleagues, children)

____ your energy at work is low—you have difficulty returning phone calls and doing your normal work activities

How many of these nineteen symptoms do you have? Would your colleagues at work rate you the same way as you do yourself? If you have at least five of these symptoms more days than not for the last two years, *you are struggling with a depressive cycle.* Your career and personal life are directly affected by this mood cycle. Who in your life knows that you are going through a depressive cycle? Make sure that, after reading this chapter, you tell your significant other or one close friend about your current emotional state. The actual power of talking to others about your secret (depression is often a silent problem) is part of the way out of this valley of despair. Remaining silent and emotionally withdrawn will only prolong the negative effects of this depressive cycle.

For many children of the passive fathering style, depression is considered a sign of weakness or something to avoid. Depression isn't a character flaw, an ethical shortcoming, or a sign of a weak personality. These perceptions of depression are outdated and a classic form of denial. A cycle of depression is a warning light in your life that it is time to change things and take different action. Many people still resist the notion that a depressive cycle is a life experience that should be addressed, not avoided. The 1950s father would never consider depression a natural occurrence or a sign of emotional neglect.

It is the degree of severity and duration of these symptoms that make up a moody/depressed personality. It is normal to feel "down" at times, as it is to feel "great" at other times, but the length of down periods should match that of the up periods. The long-term process of constantly experiencing depressive symptoms is problematic. It is important to note that the combination of negative, neglectful thinking and feeling critical of yourself (the symptoms listed above), plus resenting your place in life, will always breed depression. Depressed adults generally don't enjoy their jobs, and they tolerate poorly any change or career success. These adults don't realize that they have any power to change the direction of their careers. The biggest secret in life and in your career: *you hold all the power to change!* Regardless of how you might currently feel, the truth again is that the potential and power to change the course of your career and life rest in you.

There is a wealth of personal-discovery information for us to learn when we feel down. Our professional and personal relationships and work performance are greatly affected by our mood swings. When you are feeling depressed, it is not the time to change jobs or to terminate a professional tie, but rather to address the thoughts and circumstances that are causing your downward cycle and moodiness.

Based on my professional experience, I know that the elements of lack of motivation and fear of failure are the surface issues among children of passive fathers. Your deep sense of emotional neglect can be healed by understanding it as a root cause of your sense of isolation and moodiness. Your resulting self-defeating thoughts are the roadblocks for developing motivation and risk-taking in your career.

## CHANGING YOUR MOOD AND YOUR DIRECTION

In the third section of this book, I am going to discuss in detail how to make the necessary changes that will put your career in the fast lane. In order to adequately address the neglectful, depressive features of the passive fathering style, two roadblocks have to be removed—the fear of failure and a lack of motivation. If you have ever witnessed snowplows move snow off the road at forty miles per hour, then you can see how that approach can hold true for your career roadblocks. They must be moved, no messing around.

We have looked at the style and consequences of having a passive father:

the lack of emotional connection creates an emotional void, which, many times, reveals itself in your career as a *lack of passion, a lack of motivation, and little internal drive.* Revving up the internal driving forces begins with you and your emotional status. When you begin to recognize that neglect and depression play a role in your career, you'll come to a natural conclusion of what needs to change. Managers, CEOs, supervisors, schoolteachers, parents, coaches, and researchers all wonder why some people are motivated and others aren't and why some professionals take risks and others avoid them like the plague.

When you start to embark on the journey of changing your mood, many things begin to happen. One is you will start to see yourself in a more positive light. Self-doubt and thinking negatively about your life are the quickest ways to stay depressed and hopeless about your career. Your career motivation is directly connected to your sense of self and emotionality. If you don't engage people emotionally, it will be very difficult to motivate yourself and strive for the things you want in your career and life. Professionals who report being upbeat and not depressed are willing to take reasonable risks, pursue their dreams, and follow their career with a passion. The lack of emotional connection is the ball and chain that hinders you from developing your motivation.

It is possible to develop motivation and overcome the paralyzing fear of failure. As the adult child of a passive father, you must realize that *all significant personal and professional change starts with you.* The most valuable prerequisite for self-discovery is a nonjudgmental and openly curious state of career exploration and a level of insight that goes beyond finger-pointing, blaming, and being depressed about your choices. It would be easy for Mark and Laura to each blame their father for all the difficulties they have experienced. Gina could spend the rest of her life blaming her dad for his severe neglect of her childhood and emotional needs. But Mark and Gina are gaining a new level of awareness that has moved them to a new career position and personal level that transcends finger-pointing.

## MANAGING DEPRESSION IN YOUR CAREER

Laura, Mark, and Pat have struggled with depression and moodiness. They each have taken the following steps to open up their emotions and see that they have the ability to connect emotionally, mentally, and professionally to others. For Mark and Gina, their larger perspective gained through insights has removed their fear of failure and low motivation in the workplace. Rather than retreating from people and opportunities, Gina and Mark are going toward them.

Below is a short mental-shift list to help you start removing depression and self-neglect from your career. Make a copy of the issues on this list that you want to work on in the next fourteen days.

- All change starts with you. Only you can change what you believe is possible. Think BIG!
- Be nonjudgmental of your past, present, and future. Depressed thinking is always looking backward, not forward with a positive perspective.
- If you believe that your life is in front of you (regardless of age, circumstances, past failures), what does it look like?
- Explore possible career options that you have always considered beyond your reach.
- Avoid the blame game; you are an adult now.
- Take a different mental picture of yourself—think of yourself in terms of your potential, not what you have been told.
- Move toward opportunity (you know what to do) rather than away from it. Learn to tolerate the pressure of success.
- When you are feeling "moody," think about why it is happening. Understanding your moods is critical for your career success. Don't accept that you have no idea why you feel a certain way. There is always a clue or thought about the problem and the solution.

These steps might seem difficult because they address how you really feel about and think of yourself. Having a positive sense of yourself will start to offset the neglectful, depressed, and troubled fathering from which you evolved. Another important step is allowing yourself to have inner confidence about your career. Since you came from a passive background, where there wasn't much feedback on your life, this might seem impossible. Realizing that the most important opinion of you is your own is another career step forward. What road do you think your career should take in the next two years? How can your father's legacy be more of a positive force in your job and future? What emotions and actions do you avoid? These types of questions are focused on you taking control of your future. *Remember that if you don't take control and make changes in your internalized father factor, who will?*

For instance, it is always interesting to hear men or women say that they do not care what their father thinks of them or their career choices. Usually, quite the opposite is true. Of course, they do care deeply, but, when faced with a passive father, they feel at a loss. The key is to acknowledge that having and feeling your personal power doesn't exist outside of you, but within you. No one's opinion of you is more significant and valuable than your own, and that includes your father's. Even if your relationship with your father is not strained, consider the new idea that your life is a series of choices that you make, and no one else does.

When professionals at any corporate level sincerely start to realize their own aspirations, low motivation and fear of success—caused by the secret problems of neglect and depression—are no longer issues. When a person visualizes his past, present, and future, that becomes the foundation on which to build his career. Treating the issues of neglect and depression is the only way to properly resolve any degree of fear and low motivation in your career. It is interesting to note that a large segment of the population between the ages of thirty-five to sixty struggles with depression. Such a large incidence is likely connected to the passive fathering style that most of these adults were raised with in the 1950s through the 1970s.

*There is nothing in your father's legacy that needs to hold you back.* You wouldn't be reading this book if you weren't already moving ahead in a positive direction with your career and personal life. When people start focusing their energy on their potential and their emotional needs, the basic fears of failure and success evaporate. It is a Band-Aid approach to deal only with motivation issues and not the depressed feelings, thoughts, and ideas that are underneath them. Jim's story better illustrates how low motivation and fear of failure hindered his career.

## JIM'S TURN OF EVENTS

Jim's story starts in high school. Jim graduated with a 2.0 GPA from a small private school for troubled teens. He then attended a state university and dropped out after the first semester. Jim's father, Harvey, sent him to therapy to find out what was wrong with his low motivation and a lack of career ambition. When I met Jim, he was nineteen and had to support himself after getting a 1.5 GPA in his first college semester. He got a job working as a frozen-food handler at a large supermarket in downtown Los Angeles. Jim was the only employee under thirty years old who had no prison or criminal record. Jim realized that, if he didn't take control of his life, he would never get out of this rut. Harvey was a loving, passive father who rarely got mad at Jim and didn't know how to help his son other than to stop supporting him financially.

Jim enrolled in a local community college and started attending classes at night. In therapy, Jim began to realize that he had had a very emotionally distant relationship with his father while growing up—he could never get much of his father's attention or time. Jim had also developed a habit of smoking marijuana to reduce his depression and fear. Jim began to treat and understand his depression, which affected his ability to move into adulthood and obtain a successful career. Second, Jim realized that his marijuana addiction was self-medication for his depression and fear of the future. He stopped smoking, even though it was quite popular socially among his friends. Jim changed his self-image from being a "pot head" to a career-oriented person. That mental shift helped Jim overcome his emotional blocks and lack of motivation about his future.

Another important step Jim took was that he stopped expecting his father to be the emotional and mental leader he had always wanted and hoped for. Rather, Jim took responsibility for his own career and began to pursue it with vigor. It was the first time in his life that Jim had passion and excitement for anything. He had always been passive and fearful about any new or challenging event. He always doubted his creative ability, leadership talent, and intelligence, though he had always wanted to pursue a career in the movie business. Within two years, Jim had a 4.0 GPA and fifty-eight transferable units to the film school at New York University (NYU). Jim was accepted into the film school and graduated at the top of his class two years later.

Jim currently works for a large movie studio in Hollywood and has been a producer on a number of big films in the last two years. He is now twenty-nine years old and has evolved his father's legacy into a positive force. Jim says that, when asked about his turnaround in life, "I needed to fail so I could really understand that my father wasn't going to save me or be my emotional rock. No one was going to save me. I had to do it because no one else was going to or could. Now I still struggle at times with being motivated and confident. I work hard and believe I am creating my own luck. My father looks to me as a role model of someone who is moving forward, no longer coasting in life or passive in my career."

Jim's evolution may sound simple and easy, but it wasn't. This is a man who realized at twenty years old that he couldn't approach life the way his father did and that he had to do some serious thinking to change the course of his life. Jim recognized his depression and changed the way he thought about himself and his career. Once he wasn't depressed or scared of his future and his past, Jim knew the sky was the limit.

What's your career limit? If you weren't passive or scared about your future, what is one risk you would take? Remember, it is never too early or too late to change your father's legacy and the course of your career. Even Jim at twenty knew it was time to adjust his worldview and make better choices for his professional and personal life.

The legacy of neglect, passivity, emotional distance, and lack of passion don't have to be your personal ingredients. Rather, you can find the opposite side of the same coins and move toward passion, thriving emotional connections, high motivation, and a positive self-image and worldview.

Chapter 7

# FATHERLESS DAUGHTERS AND SONS
## Finding Your Professional Power and Position

I am so sick and tired of feeling bad about my father and myself. Kids survive things much worse than never seeing or having a father while growing up. My father's absence has been almost as important as his being active in my life. Either way, my father really had an influence on my life. I have never met my father, and that is a shame.

—Curtis, age forty-nine

I lived with my father until the age of nine, when my parents divorced. I rarely spoke to my father or knew much about him before and after the divorce. My father moved to the East Coast after the divorce. I am very angry that my father was never around. He never really knew me or cared about our family. My father remarried and had another family. We haven't spoken in years; I still miss him even though I'm grown up now.

—Melinda, age thirty-three

If you are a son or daughter of an absent father, you already know it and deal with it in your life and career. As we've discussed, the absent style of fathering can be figurative or literal. In its subtlest form, the absentee father is similar to the 1950s passive father in that he's not emotionally engaged with his children. Unlike the passive father, however, the absent father opts out of the family life and the responsibilities that come with it. He isn't merely emotionally disengaged, but he seems unwilling or worse. He has no interest in interacting with his son and daughter even on the most basic level. This father has "checked out" of the life of his children.

In contrast to the previous three fathering styles (superachiever, time bomb, and passive), the absent father takes it a step further by physically abandoning his daughter or son. We can all empathize with a messy divorce, a difficult child-custody situation, or a strained marriage, but, for many of us, the complete rejection of a son or daughter is mind-boggling. This fathering style goes beyond divorce because a significant percentage of postdivorce fathers actually become more involved with their children.[1] The absent father instigates an emotional, mental, and physical breakdown in his children—the experience and perception of paternal rejection. Regardless of your age, enduring the profound impact of your father's lack of interest, abandonment of his concern, and rejection of your life can only be likened to a missile hitting the side of a building. The psychological effect is far reaching and must be understood in the development of your career. This unfortunate but all-too-common father-son or father-daughter experience is one of the main reasons that people don't discuss their father issues. It is simply too painful and emotionally overwhelming.

Another extreme example of an absent father is the deadbeat dad. The federal government passed legislation in the 1990s to mandate the financial support of one's offspring until the child reaches eighteen. This is a social sign that the absent-father phenomenon is more widespread than any of us knew. Men who abandon their children physically and financially do more than psychological damage—they deny their children educational, cultural, and other opportunities essential to their development and future career success. Even providing financial support without emotional support tremendously damages a daughter and son. Moreover, it is harmful to be physically present (live in the same house) but emotionally and intellectually absent. These fathers have no clue about what is going on in their children's lives. One thing that these fathers completely miss, don't understand, or don't care about is the negative message that this fathering style sends: his children aren't important to him.

As Curtis stated in the quotation that opens this chapter, his father's absence has been as much a force in his life as his active presence would have been. This is a very insightful statement and accurate observation. Children who have endured the horrible road of rejection by a parent have many issues with which to contend. One of them is how abandonment breeds resentment, which leads to anger and rage. It is interesting to note that the common denominator for violent gangs is fatherlessness. These teenagers, starting at about age twelve, will act out their rage on society and on each other. The absence of a father in a child's life automatically creates a deep sense of loss, which, if not resolved, healed, and understood, will only fester. Fatherless adults will likely have the challenge of anger-management issues or violent personality tendencies if they ignore the significance of this primary relationship.

Absent fathering—from indifference to physical abandonment—will lead to a coping with profound sadness (best-case scenario) or to anger issues (worse-case scenario: violence, criminal behavior, white-collar crime). The natural psychological response to a father-son or a father-daughter relationship loss is fear, pain, and then anger to cover up the emotional and mental wound. Children of all ages who experience the loss of their fathers go through this natural grieving process. It is important to distinguish between a natural loss and a deliberate loss. A father's death is a loss, but his involuntary departure versus a voluntary exit creates a different effect on children.

## FATHERS MATTER—TWO STORIES

Allan, age thirty-eight, came to see me because he was having difficulty handling all the pressures and demands of his new corporate promotion—as head of hip-hop record division. He was a very gentle type of personality, articulate, passive but with a very strong management style. Allan was having tremendous difficulty with having to hire new staff members and terminate the old ones. I asked him about his father, and he replied, "When I was eleven years old, my father was murdered. My parents owned a corner grocery store in Oakland, California. On a Friday morning in May 1977, two men came into the store, held it up, and shot my father. I have struggled with his death since then, and I know the loss really has changed my life. Immediately at school, fifth grade, every kid was my friend, and no one ever picked on me again all the way through high school. I can't fire personnel or hire people at work. I feel their sense of loss and disappointment, and it clouds my judgment. I have been dating the same girl for four years, and I can't break up with her. I hate endings, and it usually stops me from taking action."

Allan is emotionally stuck at the point of feeling lost, confused, and disappointed, much like he was at age eleven. He isn't angry or hateful toward his father. Rather, Allan says that he feels an empty place in his heart when he thinks of his father almost thirty years later. Allan is very compassionate, empathic, and understanding of others' feelings and their challenges in life. He functions well, with the exception of his fear of disappointing others and always feeling responsible for other people's sense of loss. Allan's own sense of loss clouds his judgment and career functioning. He has a difficult time seeing others' losses and disappointments in life as not his own and not as severe as his own father-son tragedy.

I asked Allan how he and his family dealt with their loss of his father. He said, "I was an only child. I had no one to talk to about my father being gone. My mother never allowed me to cry after my father's funeral, even though I was missing him. I remember how lonely the house felt after my father's death. Every Sunday night, we would watch *Mutual of Omaha's Wild Kingdom*, and it was awful. I hated the emptiness of not having my father around. All my baseball games had fathers attending, and I had my mother. It was a tough time emotionally for my mother and me until I went to college. After my father's death, my mother had to go work full time at our local bank to support us." Allan began to resolve his issues living without a father by following the steps below and those in section 3. Although Allan's circumstances were different from most of ours, we can see how they created a huge void in his personal and professional functioning.

Melinda came to see me because she was having anger-management issues with her boyfriend and with her supervisors at work. She worked for a software company as part of the sales team. Melinda felt that her male boss was a jerk, incompetent, and untrustworthy. She never had a supervisor whom she felt was worth her professional respect. When I asked Melinda to tell me a little about her father-daughter relationship, she was visibly upset (her face turned red, and her eyes welled up with tears):

> My father moved out when I was nine years old. I only saw him once a year after that until about age fifteen to sixteen. Then we stopped all communication. His new wife, useless bitch, didn't like my brother or me. My father wouldn't pay for us to fly to his house in the summer and stay for a few weeks each year, like he promised. I didn't speak to my father until my college graduation. My mother paid for me to go to college; my father said he couldn't do it. I think the stress of raising two kids on her own killed my mother when I was twenty-five. I haven't seen my father since my mother's funeral eight years ago. I don't call, and he doesn't call either. I am furious with him for abandoning me and not talking to me. I understand the divorce,

but the no communication is unacceptable. I know I don't trust men. They are all the same, players and users. I have had my heart broken enough.

I ask Melinda how her absent father has affected her personal and professional life, and she answers, "That's easy. I have always dated men fifteen to twenty years older than me. I haven't been married, and I don't want to have any children. I don't want my kids to ever go through what I went through and felt. The older men I date are nice, generous, and very supportive of my career and me. I am kind of a "ball-buster" at work, and I think I have my anger under control most of the time. I know people at work avoid me because they are afraid of my response, which isn't very good. I am really a big softie on the inside." Melinda admits that she needs to resolve her anger about her father's leaving and not be so aggressive in the workplace. Melinda knows that her aggressive, anger-based responses to coworkers are connected to her father-daughter relationship.

Clearly, Allan and Melinda are profoundly affected by their fathers' departure from their lives, for entirely different reasons, but nonetheless they are still feeling the loss. Melinda, unlike Allan, has the additional weight of anger for losing her father's love, approval, and acceptance. Absent fathers create in their children a "paradox of feelings," which are difficult to understand and resolve. The natural psychological response to a significant loss (any parent) is fear, pain, and then anger to cover up the wound or void. Children of all ages who experience the loss of a father all go through this process.[2]

Sons and daughters naturally wonder if the untrustworthy qualities that marked their fathers' departure will also recur in their personal and professional lives. They even wonder in the back of their minds, "Will I do the same thing that my father did?" They have seen their mothers' resentment and anger toward their father because he has left her alone to raise the children. Many times, the abandoned spouse's resentment and anger extend beyond the father to all men. Since half the world is made up of men, children have to reconcile their father-child experience in order to function at their full career potential.

This paternal legacy confuses children because half of their very selves came from their father, who abdicated his responsibility of parenting and being a partner. Boys are confused by their fathers' absence because they are the sons that their mothers love, and they ask themselves whether *they will grow up to be the men whom their mothers hate*. Daughters are also confused because they wonder whether all men will love them and also leave them. Either way, children of absent fathers suffer from absence and neglect. Please bear in mind that this discussion isn't intended to make victims out of fatherless children. The only point is to understand clearly the profound impact men have on their children, and recognizing them as such a force in their lives.

## REACTION TIME

Regardless of age, children of absent fathers typically cope with their emotional pain in a number of ways. First, they may turn into overachievers, becoming the person that their fathers never were, thereby pleasing their mothers and family. (Daughters, many times, become a success to offset their father's legacy of disappointment.) Second, the sons and daughters may personalize their fathers' indifference and rejection, assuming that somehow they are at fault for his departure. Third, they may take their anger out on society and the people closest to them.

Fourth, forming trusting personal and professional relationships may become difficult for children of absent fathers. This is why so many fatherless adult professionals work for themselves or wish they did. It is difficult to trust authority figures, supervisors, or any type of higher command when your primary experience with authority was so painful and disappointing. These adults often gravitate toward self-employment because they don't want to take another chance of interacting with another man or (any) authority figure that could wound them as their father did. Many times, these professionals will not understand why they distrust, dread, and dislike any authority figures. It is their lack of insight into their father factor that plays out at work. It seems crazy to coworkers to always argue with the authority structure at work. Yet, to these adult children of absent fathers, it is simply a matter of survival and revenge.

These four reaction issues (overachieving, personalizing problems, having an aggressive attitude, lacking trust for authority) all feed into the development of the angry personality and aggressive professional approach. This anger issue is the key to resolving all four issues related to fatherlessness and parental rejection. Anger by far is the strongest deterrent to a successful career future. Whereas shame is the strongest inner feeling that derives from an absent father, anger is the outward manifestation of that deep sense of inadequacy. Angry people never feel good about themselves or their reactions to others.

## UNCOVERING YOUR ANGER AND PAIN

The following list illustrates how the four symptoms of fatherlessness feed into the creation of an anger-management problem and a sense of hopelessness. It is essential to acknowledge the sadness of your fatherlessness so you can heal your deep sense of abandonment and rejection. Doing so will allow your career and personal life to move forward. No one wants to keep reliving his hurtful past in his present life and career. Put a check mark next to each question that describes your responses, thoughts, or feelings at certain times at work, at home, and with other people. Think about these questions and consider how you might be reacting to the internalization of your absent father.

### *Absent Father Checklist*

\_\_\_\_ Do you often feel that whatever you do at work isn't enough?

\_\_\_\_ Do you fear that you aren't successful in your career?

\_\_\_\_ How much of your career is consumed by the fear that you will not make it to the top or reach your career goals?

\_\_\_\_ Have people told you that you are an overachiever at work?

\_\_\_\_ What is your biggest fear in your career?

\_\_\_\_ Do you tend to personalize the problems, disappointments, and frustrations of others as your own fault?

\_\_\_\_ Do you apologize for things that you have no responsibility for?

\_\_\_\_ Do you become overly insecure about being abandoned in relationships (personal and professional)?

\_\_\_\_ Do you fear being close to colleagues or supervisors?

\_\_\_\_ How much resentment or bitterness toward authority do you have at work?

\_\_\_\_ Do you scream and scare people when you get mad?

\_\_\_\_ Have you ever been told by a coworker that you have an anger-management problem?

\_\_\_\_ Is it difficult for you to express your anger or disappointment to friends, colleagues, and family?

___ How often have you said, "I hate my father"?

___ Do you wonder, now that you're an adult, whether you are just like your father?

___ Have you ever been involved in a physical altercation at work?

___ Have you ever argued so heatedly that coworkers were concerned about it?

___ Do coworkers, clients, and supervisors worry about your angry response to disappointments and change?

___ Do you deliberately break the rules at work?

___ Have you ever been written up for, accused of being, or were willfully insubordinate?

___ Do you intentionally create problems for your supervisors or the people to whom you are accountable at work?

___ Have you ever been described as a "difficult" employee?

___ Have you been terminated from a job because of your anger or aggressiveness toward others?

___ Would you consider yourself a "flexible" employee, supervisor, and/or professional?

These twenty-four questions are designed to illustrate some of the hidden issues of fatherlessness that might plague your career and life. If you answered over 50 percent of these questions with a yes, keep reading. If you are ever going to reach your potential, it will be without an angry approach or hostile attitude toward the world and yourself. Remember that anger is only an emotional sign that something in your life isn't working or is out of balance. Try to view your rage, anger, or resentment as informational, that something deeper in your life needs attention and concern.

Clearly, anger has many forms, such as insubordination, rule breaking, chronic arguing, aggressiveness toward others, and hatred of competition. The emotional burden of this style of behavior is the unresolved anger that is created by the emotional disappointment of being a child without a father. Even though you are an adult now, that paternal loss is significant and can't be dismissed as a nonevent. People may tell you all the time that we are all "fatherless" (that we don't have a close relationship with our fathers), and that may be true for many, but it doesn't change or heal the pain in your heart.

The goal here is to work toward resolving your anger in a productive manner because it will serve your career and your personal life. There isn't enough paper or time to explain the adverse affects of an angry personality and the long-term damage it does to people and their careers. We all know of professional athletes, business professionals, colleagues, friends, and politicians who have had their careers cut short by their anger issues.

Every week, there is a story in the news about someone losing his or her temper and bringing a gun to avenge/resolve a dispute. Unfortunately, this anger is so intense that it usually results in a deadly encounter. None of us wants this. The rest of this chapter is devoted to resolving, healing, and moving beyond our anger. Anger issues are the major roadblock for any career and personal development.

## TAKING ANGER OUT OF YOUR CAREER

Although it may not seem true on the surface, your career choices, behaviors, and functioning have all been strongly influenced by your father's absence in your childhood, adolescence, and young adulthood years. This premise seems more palpable when your relationship with your father wasn't so strained, distant, and, for some people, nonexistent. As much as you consciously reject your father's absence, you are still under its sway. Most adult children of absent fathers have a tremendous amount of unresolved anger, which, unfortunately, is usually directed toward other people, colleagues, friends, family, and themselves.

Good common sense dictates that you need to deal with your anger to avoid the ongoing emotional, mental, and professional roadblocks that it inherently creates. Your career is directly influenced and shaped by these types of emotional concerns. Anger is only a smoke screen for covering up the real injuries that your absent father caused, which is *abandonment, neglect, and rejection.* The following list will help to defuse and clarify the untapped emotional issues surrounding your father, which negatively affect your personal and professional functioning.

To help you identify and discuss your anger, this list is weighted to evoke your deeply buried feelings, thoughts, and memories that still influence your present-day life and career functioning. See how many of these items are or have been true for you.

## Abandonment Issues

- Your father's physically leaving you because of a divorce or other marital problems.
- Your father's spending an inordinate amount of time at the office, with career concerns, or on the road for work.
- Your father's spending a great deal of time and energy away from the family, pursuing personal interests rather than being with you.
- Never meeting or knowing your father.
- Your father's remarrying, starting a new family, and not including you in it.
- Your father's avoiding your attempts to contact and/or have a relationship with him.
- Having very little emotional, mental, or physical contact with your father.
- Your father's refusing to be a "father" to you and avoiding that responsibility.

## Neglect Issues

- Your father's paying very little or no attention when you had something important to say or do.
- Your father's ignoring or not noticing your requests for feedback about your personal concerns, thoughts, and life decisions.
- Your father didn't attend or know or wasn't interested in your school performances, athletic events, or school progress.
- Your father was unaware of your disappointments, celebrations, or daily activities.
- Your father didn't know any of your friends, including your best friend, or your romantic relationships.
- Your father didn't protect you from dangerous situations or harmful risks.
- Your father missed important events in your life (birthday parties, proms, graduations, award ceremonies).
- Your father was aware of the self-defeating behaviors (drug abuse, poor grades, pregnancies, running away, criminal behavior) to which you resorted in order to get his attention and love, and he did nothing.

- Nothing you did, positive or negative, could get your father's attention, concern, approval, or love.

## Rejection Issues

- Your father's refusing to express his love to you in actions or words.
- Your father's telling you to go away and stop bothering him (a pattern of rejection).
- Your father's dismissing your ideas and feelings.
- Regardless of the marital situation (married, divorced, remarried), your father didn't want a relationship with you.
- Your father wouldn't financially support you growing up, in college, or in any way.
- Your father refused to participate in your life growing up.
- Your father deliberately avoided any type of contact with you.
- In spite of your mother's best attempts, your father wouldn't be involved in your life.
- You have never met your father.

These are obviously just a few of the factors, traumatic circumstances, and situations that go into the mix of creating an angry son or daughter. It is the combination of feeling abandoned, neglected, and rejected that becomes the ball of fire in a young child's life. Years of accumulation of these painful events help create an anger. It takes a lot of maturity, insight, and courage to stop these three elements from ruining your career, personal life, and family.

Use these examples to stimulate thought about your own angry childhood memories involving your father. Again, thinking and talking about these memories is key. If you find it difficult to discuss them with a trusted colleague, close personal friend, partner, or family member, try using the following technique.

## Action Step 1—Healing Anger

Pretend that your father is in the room with you and that you have a chance to tell him about how angry you were with him when you were a child, teenager, and young adult. Don't blame him for what he did or use this exercise to vent. Instead, your goal is to communicate your feelings and thoughts with precision; you want him to fully understand exactly what he did that wounded you and how he caused you to experience abandonment, neglect, or rejection. Express to him how you felt and why you felt that way. Provide a few specific incidents that illustrate your feelings. Here is a sample role-playing expression.

> When I was a child, you made me feel like I wasn't worthy of your attention because you always had your nose buried in the financial section of the paper when you were home or you locked yourself up in your office. I felt like I didn't really matter to you. I always felt like a burden to you. After you and Mom divorced when I was seven, it was as if you divorced me, too. I hardly ever saw you or spoke to you again. I remember once I called you after my first boyfriend broke up with me in the eighth grade. You said you would call me back in ten minutes, but you never called. I have always wanted you to love me and be proud of me. It seemed that no matter what I did, I could never make much of an impression on you. I don't want to spend the next thirty years of my life being angry with you. I have already spent too much time doing that. Dad, I want you to know that I really missed you growing up. I am still envious of my girlfriends who have a good relationship with their father. I know we could have done the same.

Sarah is a thirty-eight-year-old divorced mother with twin six-year-old daughters. Sarah's husband, Frank, left her after she became pregnant. Frank mails Sarah a monthly custody check, which barely covers the girls' after-school daycare. Frank wants nothing to do with the girls and has moved out of state. Sarah is furious with herself for marrying a man who is just like her father. She is very thankful, though, for her two beautiful daughters, Amanda and Alison.

Sarah, after doing the above exercise several times in my office, began to find some relief, resolution, and peace about her absent father. Sarah found that, when she clearly communicated her thoughts and feelings about her experiences growing up, it began to help her move past the pain of rejection.

## Action Step 2—Put It in Writing

Sarah, after role-playing and having these powerful discussions about her father, thought it would be productive to put her feelings on paper. Sarah wrote a letter to her father in which she expressed her feelings, her thoughts, and her heartfelt concerns. She didn't use the writing exercise as an opportunity to blast, blame, or accuse her father of being a major life disappointment. Sarah was tired of always being bitter, resentful, and angry with her father and wanted to do something different to help resolve her painful sense of rejection. Rather, she very carefully wrote down her thoughts that she had been carrying since about the age of four.

Sarah addressed her sense of male or fatherly rejection, emotional neglect, and abandonment. She took a few weeks to write the letter. After writing it, she read it to her mother, her close lifelong girlfriend, a trusted male colleague, and me. After reading it to the four of us, she put the letter away for two weeks. She reread the letter and decided to send it to her father.

Sarah was fully aware that she might be reopening the door to a relationship with her father by mailing the letter. She knew it was a calculated risk and worth taking. Her father had never seen his granddaughters or spoken to them.

The following are suggestions and some guidelines for writing a letter to your absent father.

- Write several drafts for yourself.
- When you have a finished copy, read it to at least three important people in your life. One of them should be someone who personally knows your father (e.g., your mother, friend, uncle, aunt, grandparents, sibling, cousin, stepbrother/sister).
- Read it to someone you trust who doesn't know your father but is a close friend and supporter or fan of you.
- Read it to at least one male adult figure in your life. The reason is for the automatic transference of your father's issues onto a safe male friend, colleague, or relative. (This applies to all sons and daughters.)
- Writing this powerful letter doesn't necessarily imply that you need to mail it or to make contact with your father. This process is about moving past your painful and angry feelings and finding resolution with yourself and the feelings you have toward your father. Reconsider mailing the letter weeks or months later.
- There is no mandate to take action toward your father. The only purpose is for you to let go of the pain you've been carrying from this relationship.
- Even if your father is deceased, write the letter and follow the steps above because it will help you psychologically, emotionally, and relationally to deal with your years of pain and sorrow.

Sarah did this exercise and mailed the letter to her father. She wrote the very empathic, tearful letter shown earlier, and her father did respond immediately. (I and her entire family thought she would never hear from him.) Her father, Pete, was open to hearing about the grandchildren but didn't want to discuss the past. He felt that Sarah's letter was more than enough on their shared past. Sarah began to meet with her father when she traveled east and continued to work on her anger-management issues. She is a businesswoman for a large international corporation and has used her deep sense of rejection, abandonment, and neglect to motivate herself to overcome her painful childhood.

Sarah has recently reached an impasse in her company because of her reputation of being a female "bulldozer." In fact, Sarah is so concerned about her image that she feels that she could ultimately be let go by the company. She feels very limited by her inability to be compassionate and patient and to not react to her fatherless childhood. Since Sarah has actively explored her anger and issues concerning her father, she has seen some improvements in her relationships at work. In fact, her immediate supervisor complimented her on keeping her composure in a staff meeting when another manager accused her of being negligent with a big customer. All these changes haven't been easy or without a lot of emotional pain. But the results far outweigh the avoidance.

## Action Step 3—Take Another Look

One of the most productive ways to deal with your anger is to remind yourself that your father's legacy to you was not all negative. This vital, nonemotional point is easy to forget when the rage from past fatherlessness begins to boil and flood your memory. Blaming, hating, and resenting your father for the "bad" things he did and said will not help you have a more fulfilling career or more positive adult relationships. What will help, though, is making peace with who he was. *Only you can change the picture that you carry in your heart of your father.* If you don't change it, who will? To this end, answer the following questions about your father:

- What compliments do people give you that reflect positive traits or attitudes passed on to you from your father?
- What pieces of advice did your father give you that have turned out to be valuable?

- What is the best day you remember having with your father during your childhood? What did he do or say that contributed its being a great day?
- What were your father's strengths as a person? What were his professional strengths?
- What did you as a child admire about your father?
- What is one positive thing that your father did that has impacted you?

Few men or women had fathers who were evil through and through or who were absolutely horrible. Even if they were "bad"—absent or neglectful in the relative sense—they probably had at least a few positive fathering traits, and you likely experienced some good times because of them. These good memories, freshly revisited, can take some of the bitterness out of your feelings toward your dad. Again, I am not suggesting that you whitewash the past or lie to yourself about who and what your father was. Instead, you should consciously make sure that you are aware of both the good and bad qualities of your father. Don't expect this awareness to happen overnight, but returning to these exercises every so often will help you gradually dissolve some of the negative emotions you harbor that affect your personal life and career. Remember that making your father out to be a villain will never make your life any better or happier. There is an old Chinese proverb that says that if you hate someone (your father), you'd better dig two graves—one for that person and the other one for you!

## Action Step 4—Reducing Your Hot Spots

If your anger is going to become less and less of an issue in your career, then you must be proactive and learn what sets off your anger. This is the key to changing your career path by becoming aware of what sets you "off" in the wrong direction with your colleagues, your clients, and the people in your life. Knowing your emotional triggers allows you to avoid your father's negative influence on your career. If you can go from reacting with anger and rage in a situation, to responding and considering other options, you have gained control of your life. If you have control of your emotional life, then you are going to make better choices in all areas.

Write down on a piece of paper three or four things that always "push your buttons" at work, such as the lack of support and pay at work, clients not returning your phone calls, being left out of an important meeting, someone's rigid political views, a fear of rejection or abandonment, not getting the proper recognition for a project, or a particular colleague who rubs you the wrong way. Write down what your triggers are and what usually sets them off. Then, look at the anger scale below for how you could reduce these issues to no response, no anger, or no rage. Many professionals are astute in wondering how their behavior would come across if they rid themselves of anger. Use this scale to understand how previously heated emotional triggers can be redirected and understood.

## The Anger-Management Scale

*No Anger*: You feel neutral about the situation, person, or circumstance. You have an opinion or response but not an overt reaction. You function and feel your best at this anger level. There is no situation or personal problem you can't handle at this stage. Life may not be perfect, but it is clearly manageable.

*Mild Irritation*: You have professional and personal opinions about the issue. Your sense of rejection or fatherlessness isn't playing a role here. You have the objectivity to consider both sides of the matter and feel secure in your position on the matter. You don't want to overreact, but you could if you lose your perspective.

*Moderate Anger*: You have a strong opinion. While you are still fairly objective, your sense of security is decreasing on the issue, and your insecurity is increasing. You aren't feeling safe, heard, or understood about the issue or situation.

*Extreme Anger*: Your ability to be objective is no longer emotionally available to you. Your objectivity is not functioning; you are flooded with old, familiar feelings of rejection and abandonment. You feel trapped by this volatile emotional cycle and the situation. Unfortunately, you aren't aware that this current situation is only triggering an old wound. Your anger is 80 percent about the past and 20 percent about the present—not the other way around. It is critical for resolving your anger to remember these ratios.

The main purpose of this four-sequence list is to illustrate how your issues with your father can short-circuit your ability to function at your full capacity professionally. When these old issues from childhood flow through your mind, it is almost impossible to function or make good decisions. The precautionary work you do by understanding your "triggers" is one of the keys for completely transforming your father factor into a positive, high-powered force in your career and personal life.

The next chapter on fathering styles discusses the performance level that most of us would like to attain. Your life is much more than the feelings of anger and rage you have buried within you about your father-child experiences. Your life is about transformation and how emotional pain is one of the greatest tools for change in life. Your experience of being a fatherless child can be a very powerful tool for understanding the interpersonal complexities and struggles that everyone has at some point in his career and life. The flip side of anger is compassion and love—traits that make the world a better place and that will make your world better.

Chapter 8

# COMPASSIONATE-MENTOR DAUGHTERS AND SONS
## The Father Factor with Style

Somehow my father always seemed to make me feel important and loved. He always had a way about him that made other people feel better about themselves. I feel very lucky to have had my father raise me; he was the best, a truly great man. I still count on his support.

—Lauren, age thirty-four

My father's parents died when he was sixteen years old. He became the father he always wanted with me and my brother. There is no way I could take the business risks and do the things I do at work without my father's love and support. He has always believed in me. I am telling you, there is no one like my father.

—Jeff, age forty-eight

## THE COMPASSIONATE-MENTOR FATHERING STYLE

This father is the man that all the other kids on the street wanted as their dad. This father did things with his children that other fathers dismissed as unnecessary or didn't have time for. He spent time with his son building a model car, helping his daughter choose her college essay topic, going to student-teacher conferences. He was ahead of his time in terms of understanding his role in valuing his children's lives and in nurturing them. Professional experience tells me that approximately 10 percent of all fathers

157

make up this group of men. The other 90 percent of father-daughter and father-son relationships are described in the previous four chapters. These four fathering styles have pieces of the compassionate-mentor style, which takes the strengths of others and puts them all together. The compassionate-mentor is the prototype of the excellent manager, the compassionate executive, the prosperous business owner, and the person for whom everyone wants to work. He is not perfect or without fault, yet he finds a way to stay emotionally connected to his children, as well as colleagues, employees, and other people in his life. People crave feeling important and emotionally connected to others; the compassionate-mentor father understands these valuable needs.

This type of fathering is called the compassionate-mentoring style for many reasons. This father empowered his daughters and sons to pursue their dreams, strengths, and hopes in a healthy manner. This father understood his role in his children's lives as irreplaceable and critical to their future development. Regardless of marital (married, divorced, stepfather, other) or career status, this father was consistent in his emotional attachment as a parent, which created within his children a sense of safety, support, and a feeling that things will always work out. This constant emotional, mental, and psychological connection allowed his children to develop many useful and important qualities and skills. This father is a natural mentor to others because of his ability to empower them to reach *their* goals and dreams.

## *Elements of the Compassionate-Mentor Father Factor*

- Compassionate-mentor adults have the psychological ability, insight, and wisdom to understand, respect, and appreciate that employees, colleagues, and clients all have their own perspective about the workplace (personal/professional confidence).
- They have tolerance and acceptance of personal and professional differences. This includes religious, ethical, relational, and career disparities (understanding/insight).
- They are emotionally capable of understanding other people's feelings, thoughts, and concerns without being defensive or judgmental. They value the purpose and role of emotional attachments (emotional intelligence—insight into the emotional process of yourself and others).

- They demonstrate leadership qualities, including the ability to say no to peer pressure, regardless of the social and professional consequences (strength of character).
- They trust their personal beliefs and have convictions (self-worth).
- They pursue their own dreams and goals and take personal and professional risks (courage).
- Sons and daughters of this father feel loved and fortunate to have this father-child relationship. They are able to be considerate and understanding toward others in the workplace (compassion). They know that most adults weren't raised with this fathering style.

This inner confidence from the father is transmitted to his daughters and sons from the day they entered the world to the present. One of the most striking qualities of this fathering style is the absence of the usual "baggage" of anger, neglect, resentment, and need for approval. It is the absence of these emotionally draining and energy-consuming issues that allows for the development of positive, life-affirming qualities, which include, along with the ones listed above, self-esteem, empathy, courage, emotional security and stability, strong professional and personal relationships, and a vision for life and career paths.

The compassionate-mentor is the model for developing a positive style in your own career and personal relationships. It starts at a baseline that the world is a safe place, and your personal needs are met or will be met and things will work out. Regardless of their occupation, these sons and daughters feel good about themselves, and that is passed on to the people surrounding them in their lives. These children of a compassionate-mentor father have the insight and compassion to understand others, relate to contrary opinions, and communicate their beliefs in a positive manner. They are able to do this because this has been their example throughout their lives.

## EMPATHIC ATTUNEMENT—THE RIGHT FOCUS

When a father helps his children to separate and make their own lives, good things begin, and generally will continue, to happen for them. Paternal understanding of one's children allows his daughters and sons to develop their own feelings of love, self-worth, and a sense of competence (i.e., being capable and willing to take risks). Fatherly support, many times, makes the difference between a child's becoming a high school dropout, a chronic drug abuser, an unreliable employee, miserable at work, or a successful and accomplished adult. These differences are strikingly clear and very serious with or without a father's support, approval, and love. We have discussed in detail the seven major roadblocks in a career that derive from the absence of these supportive elements in a child's life. Now we are going to focus on what happens when these critical father-child elements (love, acceptance, empathy, and guidance) are present in this relationship. Then, we are going to examine how these elements can become part of your internalized father factor in business and in your personal life.

The first step in becoming the professional and the good parent that you've always wanted to be is to understand the role of emotional attunement (the ability to understand a person's emotional state and react to it appropriately) and empathy. The compassionate-mentor (referred to as C-M from now on) father has the intuitive nature and awareness of how to support his children in their day-to-day routines. This type of understanding, mentioned earlier, allows a child to develop feelings of self-love, self-worth, and competence. *It is important to remember that a young child's feeling of being loved is more important than how much he or she was in fact loved.* A child will naturally develop a secure emotional sense based on how much she feels loved and cared for. Children sense this by how their father consistently took time to really listen to how bad their feelings were hurt in the first grade at recess or how scared they were about going on their first overnight at summer sleep-away camp.

*The C-M father isn't perfect*, but rather he is alert to his daughter's or son's different emotional states and mood changes. Attempting to know what bothers his teenage children is critical to their mental health. Acting on this information appropriately creates a net of emotional support for them. The core foundation for all effective styles of fathering, which can also translate into management, is the ability to focus on your daughter or son as an individual rather than on a particular behavior. Emotionally bonding with your child, rather than focusing on a negative behavior, consistently sends the message that he is important to you. That proper focus allows both parties to have an ongoing open line of communication with an uninterrupted emotional connection. This is the basis for a child's developing a positive sense of his world and his place in it.

A great example of empathic attunement is the ability to join someone else in his or her state of excitement even though you might feel differently about it. When both young Lauren and Jeff (quoted in the beginning of the chapter) came home from school with a blue ribbon for being the best speller or the top kick-ball player in the class, their father shared their excitement. This type of empathic attunement fosters a young girl's or boy's sense of self-worth. This self-worth, in turn, becomes the internal confidence that allows this child to face future challenges and further her ability to trust that people will care for her. These children grow up to become adults who can share in others' successes and support their colleagues' accomplishments without feeling insecure or scared.

Because the C-M father repeatedly connected on the same level as his children, he communicated the invaluable sense of safety and love to them. We all know what a painful and disappointing experience it is when an important person (father, partner, colleague) in our life does not intuit or share our excitement about a particular task, event, or accomplishment. The emotional miss is painful and causes us to rethink whether we should share our excitement with that person ever again. Children who repeatedly experience this type of emotional disappointment with their father may eventually stop experiencing positive feelings toward him. The emotional letdown is too painful, so it may be avoided at all costs. Children of the C-M father don't carry this type of emotional wound.

Let's keep in mind that the C-M father is not without failure, moments of emotional outbursts, or negative feelings. But from an early age, his children know that their father cares about them, even if he completely misunderstands certain situations, especially if he supports them from ages thirteen to twenty-two through their mood swings and emotionally needy times. These sons and daughters know that they will have their father's guidance and love to carry them through periods of great difficulty and personal change. That recurring, unspoken support allows people to feel emotionally bonded to their father. It creates a deep sense of safety, which allows them later in life to take adventurous steps, make important choices, and tackle professional challenges. These types of courageous moves are all possible because of their father's *active support*. That sense of confidence is contagious and a great personal motivator in the workplace.

It is very important to remember that, if your father's style and your childhood don't reflect this type of positive experience, don't be disheartened or hopeless. You can create the type of professional and personal environment that will foster this confidence and inner strength within yourself and in your children. We will discuss how to do that at the end of this chapter and in the next section.

## RESPONSIVE FATHERING

The C-M style of fathering has the special feature of a positive personal history. A father's lack of emotional anger, which would have stemmed from his relationship with his father, allows him to see his children through a clear and objective perspective. This clarity is critical to being able to respond to his children's particular needs for separation, individuality, and making their own life choices, including selecting a career path. It is this father's pleasure and habit to give verbal and nonverbal support to each of his children's developing personality and sense of self—this is a man who understands the value of being emotionally, mentally, and psychologically responsive to his children at all stages of life.

A close friend of mine, Mike, told me the following story about his daughter, who is a college freshman: "Jennifer came home from her first semester at school [twenty-five hundred miles from home] and saw me and immediately started crying. I sat in Jennifer's bedroom for the next two hours while she cried about the fear of losing her safe place at home as well as her great circle of friends from high school. I had a lot of phone calls to return that night, but I knew she needed me to be just in her room with her and actively listening. I am glad I did it, and Jennifer needed to know that nothing had changed in our relationship." Mike is a C-M father and has done these kinds of things with his children for years. This example may seem trivial, but it illustrates that we must respond to our children when they need us, not the other way around. This emotional attunement, understanding, and empathic capacity are vital traits that the adult child adopts and translates into success with colleagues, clients, and supervisors.

What is really interesting about this example is that Mike was raised not by a C-M father but by an absent father. Throughout Mike's childhood, his father was addicted to pain medication. The chronic prescription drug abuse kept Mike and his father from having a close emotional connection. Mike has worked very hard to overcome his "fatherless" past, even though he lived with his father and saw him every day. Mike's father used drugs and his busy work schedule to stay away from his whole family. Mike has persevered and developed a positive C-M fathering style in spite of his painful childhood. He has used many of the exercises in this book and at the end of this chapter to become a C-M father to his daughter and son. The father factor that he has created within himself reflects his emotional and mental capacity to understand and empathize with people. But Mike, like most of us, didn't initially have a C-M style of fathering. Rather, he decided to become that kind of person at work and at home.

The C-M is a father who doesn't have a long list of unfulfilled dreams or resentments about his past, and, if he did, he has worked to overcome them. He is able to function in the present with his children and thus allows them to do the same. The sense of courage and competence of the C-M father is transferred to his child, which is the foundation that allows them both to be independent and interdependent simultaneously; they have the capacity to be separate and yet deeply connected. Adult children of a C-M don't feel the pull of their father's unfilled dreams and wishes. Those who have carried their father's disappointments, frustrations, depression, and resentments know this burden in their personal lives and careers.

It is very difficult to move forward with your career when you feel your father's resentment and jealousy about *your* professional success and personal growth. The C-M father communicates in his actions and words the freedom for his children to create their own lives with the safety net of his support and love. This does not mean that this father and child do not disagree, but rather that permission exists in their relationship for their differences. The agreement to disagree creates room for the child's (regardless of age) self-worth to tolerate rejections, disappointments, and frustrations. This father and daughter or son have learned that they can discuss hot issues— such as sexuality, money, parenting, career choices, professional growth— without having to fight for their opinions, thoughts, and feelings to be heard. They have learned to listen to and support one another, even when it is not to their personal preference. An unspoken atmosphere of acceptance is the foundation for their children's thriving and growth.

When these children become adults, their professional lives are not a miniseries of emotional "disasters" or nagging self-doubts about their ability to perform in the workplace and function at their fullest capacity. This inner confidence carries over to their adult love relationships and other important emotional connections.

## BLENDING THE C-M FATHERING STYLE INTO YOUR FATHER FACTOR

The list of qualities and emotional gifts that the C-M father gives his children is endless. It is important to understand that, if indeed you had a C-M style of fathering, there is a very high probability that your coworkers, clients, supervisors, and friends didn't have the same father-child experience growing up. In fact, people tend to resent you or feel that you have no idea of their pain, disappointment, and sometimes horrors that they lived through. That may be true in terms of experience. The lack of father-child pain, nevertheless, isn't a deterrent to your ability to have compassion for, understand, and emotionally connect with your colleagues in a powerful way. Experience isn't a necessary element for emotional understanding. Insight and empathy are often just as valuable assets.

What you experienced in terms of approval, understanding, emotional support, and love are the same things that the men and women in your job crave. We all have the same DNA wiring for these emotional needs, wants, and hopes to be responded to and developed in all of our lives. The offspring of C-M fathers have the capacity to know that people need these very important inner personal qualities. It is not very easy to be a leader to coworkers who don't believe that their leader really cares about them. You have the personal experience to know that support and approval are great motivators and very important in the workplace. You know from experience that showing empathy is the fastest way to heal and empower the people surrounding your career and life.

*Bear in mind that most people don't factor in the influence of their father into their career choices, progress, and development or their personal and professional relationships.* Fathering styles can range from the current discussion of the positive C-M experience to the extremely problematic and painful styles as seen in the last four chapters. An apparent lack of insight is completely understandable given that so many adults have had such disappointing, turbulent, or painful relationships with their own fathers. For most people, it seems much easier to avoid the entire topic of the father completely. *Wrong choice.*

The ultimate goal of this book, particularly this section, is to show the endless and seamless connections, behaviors, attitudes, and beliefs linked to your relationship with your father. No child, regardless of age, is neutral about her father or how she was raised. One of the pitfalls of discussing the

C-M fathering style and the father factor is the hopelessness, blame, and anger that can get stirred up by it. It is always valuable to keep in mind that finger-pointing and father bashing is a nonproductive response to deeper emotional wounds. Again, it is essential to always remember the old Chinese proverb that says that, if you are going to resent someone, you'd better dig two graves—one for the person you resent and the other one for you. You lose in all areas of your life when you choose to blame, resent, and rage against your father.

Your relationship with your father is merely a starting point—a baseline for the development of your father factor, *not the stopping point*. You are completely in charge and responsible for how your father factor evolves, functions, and influences your career. This is the good news because no fathering style can impair you from becoming the person you've always wanted to be with the career you have always desired. You have the power and now the insight to change your self-defeating behaviors, cynical beliefs, and negative attitudes that have stalled your career. These are bold statements about your potential, which is the undiluted truth about you and your father. I really believe that adults know on some level that their careers could move forward if a few things were changed or slightly adjusted.

Up to this point, we have spent a great deal of time discussing the various problems, crises, and neglectful and painful fathering that so many adults have experienced. This chapter has shown you that you are closer to your goals than you think. The more you understand and begin to incorporate the C-M style and its various strengths into your life, the sooner your career can move forward. In order to better understand the C-M style, consider the following set of questions. Please answer them with the first unedited thought you have.

## C-M Father Factor Questions

- What are five things that you would have liked to have done with your father prior to graduating from high school?
- What are two things you would like to do with your father now that you are an adult (regardless of whether he is living or dead)?
- What are five things you would have liked from your father while growing up (think big, not based on your emotional pain or your father's limitations)?

- What is the most important thing to you, now as an adult, in a father-child relationship?
- If there is one thing you would want from your father today, regardless of the reality of the request, what is it? (Saying "nothing" is a defensive nonresponse.)
- What limitation, trait, or weakness do you have that is directly connected to your father?
- What is one of your personal and professional strengths that is related to your father's influence?
- What one quality of the C-M fathering style would you like to use more often in your career?
- What is one of your behaviors, attitudes, or beliefs that you know you need to change in your work relationships?
- What would you like from your father in regard to your career and life choices?
- How often do you think of your father at critical moments in your day, during important career choices, and in your personal life?
- What is one thing that you have learned from your father concerning personal and professional relationships (positive or negative)?

These are very powerful questions designed to open up a personal discussion with yourself about the influence, impact, and legacy that your father has had on your life today. This discussion is similar to peeling the skin off an onion; there are many layers on top of others. The purpose of each chapter and list of questions is to keep going to the heart of your relationship with your father and its residual influence on your life up to this point. Your life is a combination of unlimited events, millions of experiences, and critical, life-changing influences.

## IT'S YOUR FATHER FACTOR

Your father is one of the most powerful forces in your past, present, and future. People know this is true but don't know what to do with the huge father-shaped hole in their heart. The pain, emotional horror, neglect, and all other father-related issues can, to a great extent, be resolved. No matter what has happened between the two of you, you must reconcile your attitude toward your father. How this takes place is a wide-open discussion and ongoing process. Ultimately, any reconciliation, healing, forgiveness, and understanding starts and ends with you. It really doesn't matter what your father thinks or does—it matters only what *you* do in your heart, mind, and actions toward him. You have to do the internal work of this recovery process. Part of adulthood are the responsibilities that come with its privileges, opportunities, and empowerments. *Your father isn't going to save your life or change your luck*; you are, and that is the truth. Most of the time, it is better not to even speak with your father about your new personal and professional changes. This cautionary note is based on my professional experience of observing people change and their fathers not understanding their need to change and evolve. This indifference, many times, is a major setback.

Don't make the common, naive mistake and assume that your career, personal, and family relationships aren't all deeply influenced by the natural occurring father-child relationship. Your father is a force to be reckoned with, and this is the time in your life to do it. (Your mother is another person who deserves your time and attention. Please see the bibliography for excellent mother-child resources.)

The C-M fathering style is the model that we all can aim for, achieve, and use productively in our careers. To attain that goal, you need to come to terms with the impact your father has had on your life. The insight, resolution, and changed beliefs have to be yours and only yours. Your feelings, thoughts, and memories can't be based on the family myth or your mother's opinion about your father, which are all important factors, but they still aren't yours. If you spend some time thinking about your father, you will be able to find the issues that need to be resolved so that you can move your life forward. Don't disregard any random thoughts about your father or things you have never considered about him. It is now the time to heal those old father-child issues.

Honestly, if you are going to genuinely change your father factor, you must start with the complete personal truth that you carry in your head and heart about your father and you. It isn't easy for a daughter or son finally to acknowledge who and what happened in childhood and how that could possibly be a factor in his or her career today. No one wants to face the truth that his or her career has gone sideways—or worse—due to repercussions from the relationship with his or her father. How many more missed promotions, low-paying jobs, daily work frustrations, and days in your career do you want to live with before facing the truth? Still, it is necessary and timely to let go of the past impediments and move forward with courage and strength and to a sense of peace and satisfaction. Before we end this chapter, consider these three questions today:

- Who was my father?
- Who am I in relationship to my father?
- Whom do I want to be in my career, in my personal life, and with my friends, family, and children?

Ponder these questions because, in the next section of the book, we are going to discuss the seven roadblocks and the seven C-M father factor traits. The roadblocks discussed in the last four chapters do have positive sides.

The next chapter is a little different from the previous eight. It focuses on the spoken and unspoken rules that you learned from your father about how to be and act in the world. The "rules" chapter is important to cover and understand before we go into the action phase of the book. We all live by rules. Do you know what the rules of your internalized father factor are?

# FATHER FACTOR AT WORK

Chapter 9

# DAD'S RULES GROWING UP

## Sons' and Daughters' Long-Term Influences

I have always lived by my father's rules. I didn't realize how many rules, beliefs, and opinions I have picked up from my father about work, money, and life. I really feel awful when I break these rules, and I don't even know what all of them are.

—Barbara, age forty-four

The whole concept of rules has always caused me problems in my career and life. My father was in the military, and my childhood was about not breaking the rules and being a good boy. I have certainly been noncompliant most of my adult life.

—Brad, age thirty-two

Following rules is like breathing: it is something we do and don't even notice until there is a problem, which, many times, is the breaking of an unspoken rule, such as always saying yes to authority figures. For instance, you say no to a request from your boss at work, and your stomach suddenly drops five floors. You are perplexed by your internal stress response to a simple yes-or-no question. You spend the next hour worried that you might have offended your boss by your uncharacteristic behavior. You resolve your anxiety by going back to your boss and telling her that you have changed your mind and that you will do the project.

Rules are part and parcel to each style of fathering we have discussed. All five fathering styles (superachiever, time bomb, passive, absent, and compassionate-mentor) have their own set of rules, spoken and unspoken. What is interesting is that most sons and daughters don't even realize the impact of their early rule-learning behavior until they violate one of the rules. Here we are going to focus on the spectrum of rules that include behaviors at work and in the career, personal and professional relationships, money, ethics, and parenting. Each one of these five areas of daily functioning is greatly shaped by your relationship with your father.

Before we go to the next section of how to incorporate the compassionate-mentor fathering style into your internalized father factor, we need to examine the rule book that you live by in your career and life. Rules are like the furniture in the family room—every piece has its place and function. The same can be said of your internal rule book. It has a practical function, exact place and specific purpose in your life. Knowing what your rules are and how they work are necessary if any changes to your internal father factor are going to occur.

## DAD'S RULE BOOK

Every fathering style has its own set of rules that every family member lives by, including your father. Some rules are passed from generation to generation of father-child relationships. Your father's rules—which compose his fathering style—influence everything from your day-to-day behavior, your choice of intimate partner, to your career. The rules ultimately affect how you behave and how you see your world and your place in it. To truly understand yourself, you have to understand the rules that govern your life. The challenge is to become acutely aware of what rules have contributed and influenced who and what you do today.

Everyone has a particular set of rules by which they live—no one is exempt from a father's legacy of rules, and that includes teenagers and adults. How many times have we all heard the rebellious, angry teenager say to his father in a heated argument, *"I am not living by your rules anymore."* The father stands there as the teenager (or adult or three-year-old) storms out of the room. The truth of the matter is that we all live, to a large degree, by our father's rules; it is a natural by-product of the father-child relationship.

One of the most important roles a father plays is that of the "rule giver." Children must learn from their parents how things work and where natural limits are in life. Another duty that fathers have is to prepare children for the adult world—which includes work/career, relationships, money, and ethics—by providing rules for these areas and how to function effectively in them and in the world at large. Children learn early in life, for instance, that touching a hot stove isn't a good idea. Most of the rules you follow today, consciously and unconsciously, are appropriate, practical, and often referred to as "common sense."

Try to remember when you questioned your father about not wanting to go to bed at 8 p.m., about brushing your teeth before school, or about wearing a jacket outside in the winter. The classic "Why?" from a child is a natural response to rules. The questioning of, wondering about, and testing of rules is a normal process that continues into adulthood. You learned from an early age what rules your father valued and how to live within those limits peacefully. Following the rules helped create a sense of safety with your father and for you and your entire family. There were—and still might be—huge emotional and psychological benefits for following the rules at home, school, and work. People respect those who follow the rules because it demonstrates strong character, as it also does to break the rules at certain times. The key is to know which rules in your life are desirable to change and which ones aren't.

All fathers live by rules. It is a given fact, regardless of your father's level of mental health and career functioning. For instance, with the time-bomb father, when someone gets upset, the unspoken rule might have been, "Immediately blame someone else; someone always screws up." An auxiliary rule might have been, "Yelling at and blaming others is normal." The passive father might have the unspoken rule, "Never show emotion," or "Adults never cry; never talk about emotions; Men don't cry." The superachiever father might have the rule, "Never fail at anything," or "Winning is the only thing that counts in life." The absent father might have the unspoken rule, "Relationships aren't that important" or "Anger is a bad feeling to have and express to others." Even though these rules are less than optimal, they are nonetheless some of the types of rules that you might have grown up with.

Think of some rules that you have learned from your father, whether they are spoken or unspoken. List at least five rules (in any area of your life) that you know you have learned from your father and that are active in your life today. It's okay to write in this book (an old rule from my elementary school was, "Never write in a book"):

1.
2.
3.
4.
5.
6.
7.
8.
9.
10.

## UNSPOKEN RULES—THE SILENT FORCE

The rules you listed are very powerful elements in your internal father factor. Spoken rules influence your life, but their power pales in comparison to unspoken rules that exist and function in the hearts and minds of all children, regardless of age. Unspoken rules are the most powerful rules in your daily life. Even though unspoken rules have enormous influence in how you function—quietly dictating your daily actions, behaviors, and beliefs—they tend to be out of your conscious awareness. Spoken rules can be laws, social norms, company policies, and codes of conduct. For example, people consciously know that drinking and driving is very dangerous, possibly deadly. It is an irrational argument to imply that the consequences of driving drunk are something that you didn't know about. In contrast, an unspoken rule, although quite questionable, might be that, if you don't drink your five daily glasses of Merlot (red wine) before 4 p.m., you aren't a problem drinker. Unspoken rules are very personal and the internal guidelines for how you relate to your coworkers, clients, and yourself.

Unspoken rules are an integral part of your core belief system of how you function in every area of your life. These, unspoken beliefs were learned in your childhood by observing your father or noting his absence. Children have a nonstop camera running in their mind, recording any and all behaviors, comments, and attitudes of their parents. Fathers tend to dismiss this natural phenomenon and its influence. If you grew up with the absent fathering style, you still learned plenty of unspoken rules about relationships, children, men, work, and emotions. Below are a few examples of ways of behaving and unspoken rules that children have learned from their fathers. These rules were passed onto you and contribute to much of your current behavior in business and in personal relationships.

*How do men and women act around one another?* Do you become assertive, passive, or submissive? Do you ask for what you want, or do you wait for the other person to figure it out? Can you express your desires to others, or do you consider that being selfish? Do you believe that men and women can't be friends without having a physical relationship, romantic encounter, or sexual tension between them? Do you believe men and women are wired differently in terms of career functioning? That men and women can never peacefully coexist together in the workplace?

*How do women act around other women?* Do you have to compete with other women for attention, love, and recognition from men (the absent father influence)? Can women ask for what they want and not be viewed as aggressive or "bitchy"? Is it appropriate for women to succeed in business and be more successful than men? Can you trust other women? Will women support you? Do "good girls" have fun, or are they always serious about business? Is talking about men and relationships very important for a woman?

*How are men supposed to act around men?* Do you have to brag about your job, income, career path, and athletic abilities to have male support and approval? Do you believe that men are always competitive and aggressive with each other? That men don't cry or show "soft" emotions and feelings to other men? That you should never tell a woman that you care more for her than she does for you? Do you think that you should never allow a colleague to know about all your secrets, abilities, and professional connections? That being a "successful" man means having enormous wealth and a high social position? That men will respect only money and power? That most men aren't trustworthy and should be kept at arm's length?

*How should you feel about your work, career, and colleagues?* Can you enjoy your work and value what you do? Do management authority figures always take advantage of your abilities and talents (the passive father influence)? Is work the most important thing in your life (the superachiever influence)? Should women love being mothers more than having careers? Are men defined only by their successful or failed careers? Should adults have fun or enjoy their careers? Can you be fulfilled by what you do, or do you work just for a paycheck?

*How should you feel about money?* Do you believe that making money is the only reward in the workplace? That money isn't the root of all evil or corruption? That people should be compensated for their work, ideas, and value to a company (the compassionate-mentor father influence)? That no one should pursue only money in their career? That men should make more money than women because they have to support their families? That women should never ask for a raise or be money smart? That women shouldn't compete with men for money, power, or rights (the passive father influence)? That making money is an acceptable and worthwhile endeavor to embrace (compassionate-mentor influence) in your career? That worrying about money matters is normal?

*How should adults feel and think about their sexuality?* Can you take pleasure and comfort in your sexuality? Should women never be assertive in a relationship about sex? Should men always pursue a partner sexually (superachiever influence)? Should your sexual partner know what you like or don't like without having to discuss it? Do you feel ambivalent about your sexuality? Do you feel comfortable about expressing your sexual orientation? Do you think that communication about sexual matters isn't very important or necessary because no one talks about sex?

Whether or not a father knows it, his children are always watching him for their entire lives. A father's behavior becomes a person's basic instruction manual on how to function in the workplace, the world, and in life.

If you were an outsider observing the impact of the unspoken rules from your father on the members of your family, you might think that you were watching an elaborate play, clearly orchestrated by an unseen director. These rules that were communicated by your father to you and your other family members, automatically became part of who and what you are and why and where you go in life.

The major problem with unspoken rules is that they are unspoken beliefs that guide your life. The majority of unspoken rules are fine, productive, and important to maintain in your life. Let's focus on the core rules, spoken and unspoken, that currently guide *your* internal father factor and include your career, relationships, money, and ethics. Again, write in the book some of our conscious and unconscious rules, beliefs, and behaviors that you follow in these areas:

Career/Work—What are your feelings and thoughts about your current job? What is one rule that guides you at work? What is a belief that you have about your career that feels special to you? Do you believe that you are in the right career for you? If not, what career would better suit you and your talents? Do you believe that a workaholic approach to your career is the only option? Which one of these five terms would best describe your approach to work: persistent, determined, relaxed, bored, or driven?

Relationships—How important are personal and professional connections, friendships, and colleagues to you? What is your definition of a good professional relationship? Can you be yourself with your coworkers? What purpose do personal relationships have in your life? Who is your best friend currently? Do you have the same type of relationship with colleagues or subordinates that your father had with you? Who was your father's best friend when you were growing up? What did you learn from that relationship?

Money—What did you learn from your father about money? Second, what did you learn in your childhood about spending and making money? Do you have emotional issues surrounding money, such as guilt, fear, deprivation, and anxiety? Do you worry about not having enough money? Are money matters a topic to be discussed? What were the attitudes in your childhood home about money matters (parental tension, arguing, indulgence)? Are you generous with your money, time, and emotions? Can you ask for a raise?

Ethics—What secrets do you carry about your father, family, and yourself? Was your father an honest man? Do you privately consider yourself an honest person? How important is your integrity and honesty with coworkers, friends, your partner, and your children? What did you learn about being ethical at work from your father? How often do you cut corners, take shortcuts, or tell "white lies" to colleagues, clients, or supervisors? Do you value the importance and role of ethics in your life?

We have discussed many types of fatherly rules that are connected to your father-daughter or father-son relationship. The primary question of this chapter is, *What rules do you feel must change in your career and life?* It is very easy to change a rule once you recognize it as something that isn't immovable or beyond your reach. The problem usually isn't in changing a rule but rather in the emotional connection it has to your father. Many of your childhood rules, both spoken and unspoken, are easy to change when you observe them as no longer useful in your life. The key is to find out the unspoken rules that govern your internalized father factor. This investigation into rules that are consciously or unconsciously running your life is well worth the effort and the emotional pain it might trigger.

The third issue (the first being your father's rules and the second, unspoken rules) comprises the emotions tied to breaking, changing, or not following any longer your outdated rules. This becomes challenging for many professionals because change tends to evoke anxiety, fear, and other uncontrollable feelings and thoughts. For instance, it takes courage to change how you relate to authority figures if your father was very verbally abusive with you (e.g., the time-bomb father influence). The fear of not pleasing people is another very common rule that causes many careers to stall out or get derailed (e.g., the superachiever father influence). You can't please everyone, and that requires your new ability to tolerate the feelings of change.

## CHANGING THE RULES—WHY AND HOW?

Breaking or changing your rule book is critical to putting your career in the fast lane. There is no way around changing your father factor without implementing some significant changes in how you view yourself, your coworkers, and your career. Those perceptions, beliefs, behaviors, and attitudes are all tied into your personal rule book. *The rule book comprises your attachment style, all the aspects of your own style, your career beliefs, and, of course, your father's rules.* Each of these areas is significant and related to how you behave, act, think, and feel at work every single day. We all have bouts of semi-amnesia and forget that we are the total of all these factors while we are stuck in rush-hour traffic, late for a meeting, searching for new clients, debating about parenthood, or meeting a deadline to close a business deal. Our personal rule book guides all these daily events and decisions.

In psychology, change is considered the most challenging task any adult can ever attempt. Amending and updating your personal rule book can cause you to have panic attacks—sudden hot flashes, a rapid heart rate, shallow breathing, incoherent thoughts and feelings, and a fear of dying. The primary underlying psychological cause of panic attacks is the perception of losing control. Other physical and emotional symptoms of change are a depressed mood, weight loss or gain, sleeplessness, irritability, loss of concentration, angry moods, and surges of fear. Altering your thoughts about how things should change in your life can trigger these alarming and uncomfortable emotional and physical reactions.

The reason for such strong emotional and physical responses is that you are reaching into the heart of your safety zone (unconsciousness) and moving the furniture around or maybe throwing out the old stuff (rules) and putting in new furniture (rules). You pick your metaphor, but the truth of the matter doesn't change. *Updating your rule book is necessary.* This step has to happen in your career. There is an old business adage that overnight change takes fifteen years to happen, though incremental changes can be made much quicker.

Try to be patient with yourself about the process of change and transforming your career. The steps you take may make the difference between your career fulfillment or career demise. Your most important first step is, *Ignore the cynics.* Pessimism, negative thinking, fear of change, and your current comfort zone all rebel against changes to the rule book. It is never too late or too early to make changes in your career, life, and relationships. Age, gender, past career missteps, and professional and personal relationship disappointments are motivations for change. Your prior behavior isn't a death sentence or a guarantee that you can't make the decisions that will propel your career forward. Your personal and professional history isn't always the best predictor of future success or the lack of it. Rather, your new choices and thoughts are the better career indicators for success. Consider the following steps as a guide to beginning a sincere examination of your rule book and its impact on your internalized father factor. Don't be surprised if you have guilt about changing the rules.

## THE ACTUAL RULE BOOK

The following steps are part of the larger picture of evolving your father factor in the direction that you desire. This evolution is centered around your life and all the areas connected to it—career, personal and professional relationships, attachments, money, family, and your sense of well-being. Take a minute and imagine the following. (Again, it is fine to write in this book—this is part of your new rule book).

- If you were holding your personal rule book in your hand right now, what would it look like? (Big, pocket size, leather cover, paperback, torn, used, under lock and key, etc.)
- What color is it?
- Do you carry it all the time with you at work?
- Has your partner ever read it?
- When was the last time you wrote in this book?
- How many pages are in it?
- What is written on the cover, or is it blank?
- Do you tell your coworkers about your rule book?
- What is written on the title page?
- What is the first rule written in it? Do you follow it? Is this rule still useful in your career today?
- What is written on the last page of your rule book?
- Are there any blank pages in this book?
- Whom is this book dedicated to? Why this person?
- What is the most important rule that you would like to change or disregard?
- Name one rule that you have to keep.
- What rule would you like to add to this book?
- How closely do you follow the spoken rules in your book?
- What unspoken rules do you now know aren't beneficial to you today?
- What unspoken rule scares you to change in your personal relationships?
- What one rule do you wish your father had in his rule book?

## APPLICATION OF THE NEW RULES

It is important to visualize your rule book. Most adults welcome the idea that they can change some of the rules that limit their growth and opportunities. Now that you have begun to picture this nuclear-powered force in your life, consider the following ten steps in taking action to rewrite your rule book.

Don't dismiss these steps as unnecessary or something you can do later. Now is the time. You wouldn't still be reading this book if you didn't want to change your father factor. Your personal rule book is of more value to you than your peripheral accomplishments (e.g., formal education, career position, business connections) and natural talents. Your rules dictate how you are going to maneuver through your life and your career, how you will act around the people you love, and how you are going raise your children. Finish what you started. It's your own book now!

Step One: What are the five rules (you can change as many as you wish, but don't overwhelm yourself with a completely new rule book) that you need to change? It will take time, patience, repetition, and persistence to change your behavior. What are the rules that need to change first and foremost? *Consider for a moment the magnitude of how you are changing the course of your life.* Thinking about the various changes is very empowering and motivating. Be persistent about implementing the rule changes.

Step Two: By looking at and critically thinking about how you are going to change your approach, you are pushing back the barriers that have restrained you for years.. This process is about how you function in the workplace and in your overall life. This is about no one else but you, not even your father. It is about a few rule changes that will move your life forward. Don't be alarmed by the sense of loss and discomfort that you may feel for stopping a certain behavior and starting a new one. If your motivation is low during this change, don't worry—your energy will return.

Step Three: Tell someone supportive, whom you trust, about the five rule changes you are making today. Be very specific about their nature. Explain in detail to your friend why these changes are necessary and so important in your life and career.

Step Four: Seriously consider the results of how these changes are going to positively impact your career. This includes all the different types of relationships you have, professionally and personally. Imagine how things can change in your life by your becoming more proactive.

Step Five: Make a timetable and a checklist for changing these rules and their proper implementation. The more specific you are, the better. Daily, weekly, or monthly updates are great for the application and the creation of new rules. Give yourself time to absorb these behavioral and attitude changes.

Step Six: Write down all the changes in the actual new rule book you are creating. This book can be a diary, journal, or three-ring notebook. Please make sure it is an actual book inside which you write down these career-enhancing changes. Embracing change sets yourself up for success. Remember that taking the time to form a plan makes success attainable for you.

Step Seven: For the next few months, carry this actual book with you at work in your briefcase or someplace where it is secure but readily accessible during work hours. You will be surprised by how many more thoughts, beliefs, feelings, and ideas will start to come to your mind, now that you have opened up your unspoken rule book. Your unconscious mind will reveal many new thoughts and ideas over the next few months.

Step Eight: Patience, patience, and patience. There are more reasons than pages in this book for you to practice being patient with yourself during this life and career transformation process. Think of it as if you were remodeling your home. Everything gets dirty, dusty, and moved around while your house is enlarged and expanded. Your internal life is no different. Change can be messy, but eventually your life will return to an even balance and improve.

Step Nine: Expand on how some of your existing rules could be even more functional and productive in your life. Don't limit yourself just to your career, but consider your love life, family, finances, hobbies, ways to spend your weekends, and body.

Step Ten: Even if there are only a few rules that you want to amend, do these steps anyway. This process is about change, not about competition or beating the other person. Remember that you are participating in your career. You are not a victim. No one is going to save you. Your father isn't going to save you; it isn't his role or responsibility. You are going to turn your career around and head in the direction that you have always wanted. This is all about you! This is one investment that you don't want to skip or have someone else handle for you.

Consider for a minute how the outcome of many sporting events have been affected by the serious application of the rules of the game. Professional sport teams have lived and died by the close call of a referee or an umpire following the game's written rule book. How many unspoken rules apply to playing the game of golf? It takes years of playing to know and fully understand all the different rules of etiquette that apply to such a seemingly simple game. At work, for women particularly, there are, right or wrong, thousands of unspoken rules on how a woman should act in the office. Consider all the spoken and unspoken rules involved in a wedding rehearsal, ceremony, and reception. These are the types of rules that everyone knows about or at least acknowledges that these rules do exist, regardless of whether they disagree on what the rules are. Two questions: 1. What are your rules? 2. Do these rules currently work in your career?

Chapter 10

# GETTING YOUR COMPETITIVE EDGE
## What's Your Style's Strengths?

I have always been shy and fairly passive about my career. My father was a bulldog, and I didn't want to be like that with people. I have been the opposite way, but I am getting nowhere in my career, and I need to change it.
—Jean, age thirty-three

It was only a matter of time before I connected all the dots about my career with my father's absence. My father was absent from my life, and that has always pushed me to become the man he wasn't to me and my family. The problem is I am far too competitive with everyone that I work with and know.
—Kyle, age forty-four

We have discussed, examined, and explored the various ways your internal father factor has developed up to this point in your career and adult life. If we had to summarize all our facts, insights, styles, rules, and wisdom in two words, they would be *fathers matter*. Your father matters in ways that you might not even consider. The goal of this entire book is to get you, as an adult professional or not, to move in the direction that you have always wanted in your career, life, finances, and relationships. This movement requires you to begin to uncover the mystery buried within you about your father and his highly influential effect upon your life, past, present, and future. There is an old adage that it takes only three or four logs to hold up the entire river full of logs. It is now time to focus on those few logs—your father factor issues that hold up your life.

185

These issues, your style, and approach to life are now ready to be addressed and changed. This section of the book isn't about a self-help program. This is all about deep psychological, emotional, mental, and personal changes that you have anticipated making for years but haven't quite known how to accomplish. Changing your father factor needs to start on the inside with your mind, heart, and inner life and later move to your outside world. There are very few things that will be untouched by the paradigm shift. Let's consider the following questions about your father's style, its effect on your approach, and the strengths and weaknesses of that approach. It is always worth mentioning again that all five fathering styles have inherent strengths and weaknesses.

## FATHERING STYLE ROADBLOCKS

When you read the previous chapters on the five different fathering styles, which one really spoke to you and described your childhood experience? Reflect on the five styles—time bomb, superachiever, passive, absent, and compassionate-mentor. If you need to review the chapter that best described your father-child experience before answering these questions, then by all means do so. Consider the following questions, and see how your answers provide more valuable information and practical insight into your career:

- What was your father's primary style while you were growing up?
- How does your career reflect his style in terms of your resultant behavior, beliefs, and relationships?
- Which of the seven roadblocks (*shame, self-doubt, avoidance, motivation, personal responsibility/ethics, anger, fear of failure*) is the most active behavior pattern in your career as a result of your father's style?
- What is the primary strength that you have in your career?
- What rules do you keep that are connected to your father's style?
- What is one thread from your father's legacy that runs through your entire life? (Remember, there are several threads/behaviors)?
- What attachment style (intermittent, avoidant, depressed, or consistent/secure) is the closest to yours? Do you have different attachment styles that you use in both your professional and personal life?
- What self-defeating behavior, problem, or recurring issue plagues your career and personal life?

- What is one weakness that you want to change in your internalized father factor?
- How have you used the style you adopted from your father in your personal, professional, and romantic relationships?
- What fathering style would best describe how you handle your relationships at work?

These eleven questions are designed to illuminate the common threads that run throughout your career, personal life, and love relationships. Each fathering style carries a tremendous amount of influence in how you function in the workplace. *Regardless of the company you own, the two thousand people you supervise, your managerial or other position, these early-childhood learned behaviors impact your professional functioning today.* Each of the five fathering styles has particular side effects, and knowing the negative and positive effects can greatly reduce the symptoms and problems in your career. Let's look at, first, all five fathering styles, their potential negative side effects, and their untapped core strengths. Second, how can these strengths and roadblocks, once successfully resolved, move your career with more energy in the right direction?

## WHAT'S YOUR FATHER FACTOR STYLE?

The *superachiever* fathering style emphasizes appearances, accomplishments, and behaviors that "always look good." The pressure to achieve is incredible. With your father, you always felt an undercurrent that you had to measure up to his standard, or you sensed your father's powerful disappointment. No children want to disappoint their father. The result of this performance-based relationship is the development of shame, which is considered one of the most negative forces in an adult's life. It can paralyze anyone at anytime, regardless of position, power, and finances. Shame is the result of never feeling that you are "good enough" or that what you do is "good enough." These feelings of inadequacy are therefore overwhelming—starting in elementary school and continuing as you move forward in life—and develop into a full-blown fear of failure. The emotional pain of a perceived setback is almost beyond comprehension because the ongoing feelings of shame flood your outward experience. Out of pure survival instinct, you avoid any type of risk or challenge.

*Shame and a Fear of Failure versus Insight and Understanding*

The removal of shame and fear of failure from your career requires the implementation of insight and understanding. The interpersonal qualities of insight and understanding are the hallmarks of the compassionate-mentor fathering style. Shame clouds your ability to have insight and understanding about coworkers, colleagues, and clients. Second, shame hampers your ability to function and to see your actions, choices, and ideas clearly. You may be consumed with these feelings at critical times, thinking that maybe "I'm not good enough, smart enough, rich enough," and so on in any situation. Shame always leaves you with the deep, uncomfortable sense that you simply aren't enough. This applies to your intelligence, professional capabilities, relationships, appearance, cognitive abilities, and finances, and it isn't limited to only these areas. Unfortunately, shame is all encompassing of your actions, feelings, and thoughts.

A great example of a daughter of a superachiever who transformed her life is Vera. At age seven, Vera continued living with her father after her parents divorced. Vera's father, Randall, was a college professor at a prominent private university on the East Coast. Randall remarried when Vera was nine years old. Janet was the prototype of the wicked stepmother from the Cinderella story, according to Vera. When Vera entered high school, the tension between her, her father, and Janet reached unbearable heights. Randall was furious with Vera for getting below a C average in her sophomore year. Her lack of respect for academics, achievement, and appearance sent her father into a rage. She was kicked out of her father's house in the summer of 1990 and was told never to return. Randall didn't speak to Vera for eight years.

It took Vera until graduate school to recover fully from the crushing emotional blow of losing her father's love, support, and approval. This was based on Vera's not having her father's superachieving values, rules, and beliefs as a teenager. But something happened to Vera internally at the end of her second year at San Francisco State University—she realized that her sense of shame and perceived inadequacy was, after all, *her* problem and not her father's. This insight immediately changed her grades, her sense of self, and the direction of her life and career. Vera saw that her sense of shame, her fear of failure, and never feeling good about herself were unfair. She felt bad for disappointing her father, but that didn't imply that she wasn't capable, valuable, and a "good enough" student or daughter.

Vera worked very hard in the next two years of undergraduate school to earn an A average. This effort got Vera accepted into a very good law school on the West Coast. Vera realized that her father's rules for performance, achievement, and always appearing perfect were his rules, not hers. Though she strove for an A average, this was for herself, to enable *her* to follow the profession she chose. Vera also discovered that she could spend the rest of her life hating her father and stepmother from hell, or she could gain some valuable insight and understanding into her approach to life. Today, Vera's style is more along the lines of the compassionate-mentor model. Vera knows the importance of emotional support and understanding in relationships and the workplace. Currently in her fourth year of practicing law, Vera has removed the roadblock of shame and fear of failure from her adult life. Drawing on the strengths of her father's superachieving style in her career and personal life, Vera is incorporating these talents, but with a more compassionate approach to problems, clients, colleagues, and friends.

## The Strengths of Children of Superachiever Fathers

- They have a strong work ethic and know the value of commitment to a career or to a professional course of action.
- They value hard work and are willing to take on new challenges, change jobs, and make the right career moves.
- They understand the role of achievement and setting goals professionally and personally.
- They have a persistent attitude and belief system and don't give up easily on anything.
- They have a rigid rule book for success and achievement—but can motivate others.
- They know how the workplace's unspoken rules operate and can successfully follow them.
- They can be great motivators of others by setting the example of accomplishing difficult things.
- They have a fearless quality and approach to business and work.
- They have leadership potential if there is a balance of achievement and appearance and success.
- They have an entrepreneurial spirit and drive to start a company and can turn an idea into reality, raise funds, and make investments.

The *time-bomb* style of fathering produces children who need to overcome their fear and avoidance of feelings and conflict. Children raised by this type of father were traumatized by the constant instability of their father's mood swings. The unpredictability of your father's mood swings, reactions, and untimely explosions, all of which had the entire family on edge every night. Those with this type of father learned very quickly how to "read" people and their emotional states at any given moment. This talent was a life-saving gift, given their father's incredible moodiness, constant screaming, and abusive behavior. *If you are an adult survivor of a screaming father*, you have survived many types of abuse, two of the worst being emotional and mental. You struggle with anxiety, avoidance, and fear of the future. At other times, you have self-confidence about your abilities, natural gifts, and professional talents.

## Avoidance versus Self-Confidence

The challenge in your adult life is trying not to always seek out security, safety, and refuge. All your relationships, romantic partners, business decisions, and career choices reflect your very safe and overly cautious approach to the unknown. Your father was very inconsistent in his emotional response to you as a child. The instability taught you to make an internal promise to always make safe choices. Many years later, you unconsciously avoid any and all potentially high-risk endeavors. The problem is everything in your life feels like a risk and something to be avoided. Your anxiety has developed to such high levels that your first response to the unknown is *no!* You prefer to stay in a dead-end job, a bad relationship, and anything that feels remotely comfortable, familiar, and safe.

You have learned to avoid conflict and communicating your thoughts, since you fear that, if you do, something "bad" will happen. The idea of expressing your true thoughts to another person is very uncomfortable and seldom done. It is much easier to be a "people pleaser" and do what the other person wants. This pattern of relating has you wondering what you really want in your life. Thus, you have developed this style of relating as a result of your traumatic childhood. Making commitments is also very scary because they can cause you to be emotionally vulnerable. You prefer to be isolated and "safe," which has been your pattern from your childhood up to the present day.

Mario is an adult son of a time-bomb father, Lou, who has transformed his life. When Mario was growing up, Lou would come home from work every day and physically beat the kids if the house wasn't clean. Mario, the oldest child, would take a pair of scissors and cut the edge of the front lawn so it was perfect. Lou had a drinking problem and would randomly become violent and aggressive with Mario and his siblings. Mario learned how to defuse Lou each night by keeping the house immaculate, the yard spotless, and his siblings in their bedrooms. Mario could read his father's face and knew within fifteen seconds how the evening was going to go. He was anxious every day at school, anticipating his father's nightly arrival and reaction to the family. This constant distraction caused him to do poorly in school, and it created a negative self-concept about learning and achievement.

Mario graduated from high school with a C– average (1.5 GPA). He was more concerned with keeping the peace and feeling safe at home than with being a good student. Studying wasn't an option because the chaos at home was all consuming and an ongoing nightmare for the entire family. Mario got married at age twenty-five and began attending community college. Twenty-five years later, Mario is a physical therapist who owns several therapy clinics. Still, Mario has had communication problems with his wife, Linda, and with fellow employees. He would much rather avoid an emotional conflict than get upset with the other person. When someone got angry with Mario, he would panic because of his unwritten rules about anger, which he learned from his father. Mario's rule book said that, when someone was upset with you, your life was in danger, and bad things would inevitably happen to you. Mario has since rewritten the rule: "When people are upset, my life isn't in danger, and it isn't my responsibility to always fix the problem. Anger is a natural emotion and not something to fear."

Mario has also struggled with drug abuse but has overcome it in the last ten years. The power of avoidance caused him to use drugs to numb and forget his childhood legacy and abuse. Despite Mario's difficult childhood, he has found a way to move beyond his roadblocks and live healthier— mentally and physically—in both his personal and professional lives.

## Strengths of Children of Time-Bomb Fathers

- They have excellent people skills (communicator, manager, personnel).

- They understand the workplace and know what an individual's professional needs are mentally and emotionally.
- They are highly attuned to change and the personal struggle that it causes in a person's life and career.
- They know the value of proper and appropriate communication without the use of anger or display of volatile emotions.
- They avoid abusive language, a negative work attitude, and aggressive behavior toward others and within themselves. They know how to diplomatically defuse emotionally charged incidents in the workplace.
- They are wonderful with handling and managing problem employees, clients, supervisors, or family members.
- They make excellent human resource people and personnel motivators.
- They know the emotional need that all adults have for a stable, safe, and comfortable work environment in order for maximum productivity and success.
- They know the importance of acting proper and respectful and behaving professionally with colleagues, clients, and employees.
- They understand the rules in the company for professional ethics and the responsibilities of each work position.
- They are very intuitive, perceptive, and insightful with people at all levels of the workplace.
- They understand being a "victim" to aggressive authority figures and have compassion for individuals in these types of work circumstances.

Now let us recall the *passive* fathering style. This father worked, came home, and went back to work the next day nonstop for forty-five years. He never had a motivational or work ethic problem—in fact, he was a model of consistency in his career, parenting style, and personal and professional relationships; he understood the value and purpose of commitment in everything he did or tried. The major credo of this fathering style is, *he showed his love through his actions, not his words.* Sons and daughters of this father know that he loves them, but they still have the emotional need to hear the words, "I love you and support you," which are rarely, if ever, forthcoming. It hurts all children, regardless of age, never to hear those types of supportive, caring words. This emotional gap with the passive father and his children creates many potentially dangerous roadblocks. Some of the common father factor roadblocks are a sense of neglect (personal and professional), depression, interpersonal communication problems, self-doubt, and a lack of motivation/passion.

This 1950s model of the emotionally distant father–child relationship is still a very popular dynamic today. Children of this style don't understand why their father keeps an emotional distance from them. This trend of not sharing thoughts or feelings in the family has, in fact, become a very strong paternal legacy over the last one hundred and fifty years. This lack of emotional, mental, and psychological feedback leaves these children feeling unloved, neglected, and passionless. Our father's attention and affection need to be communicated verbally and nonverbally so that we know that we are important to him and the world. Without this type of support, it is very difficult for many people to feel strong in their careers.

The need to be committed, passionate, and emotionally engaged are the main problems for these adults. The absence of these feelings breeds self-doubt and a lack of motivation. Without the passion and emotional commitment to your career, yourself, and your relationships, it is very difficult to feel motivated and to move forward in these vital areas of your life. Your life may look good, but you feel that something is missing—an emotional connection to the things you do.

## Lack of Motivation and Self-Doubt versus Courage and Strength of Character

We discussed in the first section of the book the invaluable role that relationships have in all aspects of a person's life. There is nothing you will do that doesn't require the use of relationship skills and knowledge of their application. Your career potential lives and dies with your ability to be passionate or tendency to be passive, respectively. The emotional void you may have in your relationship with your father reveals itself many times in other relationships as a lack of passion, a lack of interest, or little internal drive and desire. Still, all these outward perceptions of you by your colleagues, friends, and employees are, to some degree, incorrect. Your public demeanor doesn't properly represent your true intentions and hidden ambitions.

Your public persona can be changed because your core strengths and potential are untapped. The flip side to your lack of passion in your daily work, nagging self-doubts, neglectful feelings, and depression comprises courage and strength of character. The latter is the ability to make an emotional and mental commitment to someone, something, or yourself and to keep that commitment. Courage breeds not only commitment but also passion for a project or a particular course of action. These two qualities are the core strengths of your father factor along with the others listed below.

We met Gina in chapter 6. Her dad practiced the passive fathering style, and she consequently suffered from feelings of severe paternal neglect. Gina has struggled most of her adult life with depression and self-doubt. She has worked very hard to overcome her passivity toward her career, love relationships, and herself. Gina got married four years ago and knew if she made a commitment to a partner—someone she really cared about—her self-doubt would be considerably reduced. She is now a mother of an adorable two-year-old daughter. Gina admits that motherhood has taught her so much about being engaged and active with her child and husband. She is torn between being a full-time mother and a full-time business professional. She is concerned that her daughter, Kimberly, might experience the same type of parental neglect that she did because of her two careers (mother and business woman). Gina is very active in her career, works from her house three or four days a week, and is home every night. She is finding a way to make her career work around being a full-time mother, her top priority. To set up the type of life she wants, she has had to draw on her inner reserves of assertiveness and action.

Gina has worked very hard to more directly communicate her feelings, thoughts, and needs with her husband and colleagues. She isn't following her father's style of being passive and distant from her daughter or husband. She is aware that her husband would be more than willing to do the bulk of the parenting for Kimberly, but she does not want that. Gina's new commitments in her personal life (marriage, motherhood) have, ironically, propelled her career forward. The passion and motivation that they have aroused have also worked for her career. Her example reflects the inner gifts that a child of a passive father can discover. These inner strengths come in response to reacting against the style of the father.

## The Strengths of Children of Passive Fathers

- They understand the importance of commitment in excelling and developing a stable career and life and meaningful long-term relationships.
- They have a balanced mental approach to volatile situations, new challenges, and changes.

- When emotionally engaged with the subject matter, they have the capacity to be excellent communicators.
- They display natural leadership qualities in the workplace and home—they have commitment, vision, and goals. They are stable, consistent, and patient.
- They value the importance of people as more than just employees or colleagues.
- They exhibit a relaxed approach to problems and challenges and allow others to feel supported and safe through their calm demeanor.
- They aren't easily rattled—they don't get upset quickly in stressful situations or in crises.
- They have a positive attitude and display it to everyone in the workplace.
- They are very reliable and faithful to coworkers, friends, and family.
- They have a sincere, honest approach to problem solving and personnel issues.

One of the most troubling of all the fathering styles is that of the *absent* father. This type of father creates a host of problems in his children. In chapter 8, we discussed at length the numerous psychological problems (rage, hatred, aggressiveness) an absent father creates. The most painful one is anger, which is the quickest way to send your career, marriage, parenting, friendships, and life spiraling downward. People are scared of the "angry employee" syndrome in the workplace, at home, and in public. The surest way to stop your career from going upward is to become enraged and act out your aggressive impulses.

Anger is a natural response to a deep emotional wound that hasn't been resolved in fatherless children. These same neglected children can carry their resentments into adulthood and into the workplace. Despite having this type of father, your legacy nevertheless *can* change, and the collateral damage that has occurred. You can overcome your own resistance to change and move beyond the point of pain and roadblocks caused by anger.

Managers, colleagues, coworkers, partners, children, schoolteachers, and neighbors dread dealing with an angry employee, client, or friend. Anger is only a signal of deeper, unresolved emotional issues. Untreated anger can manifest itself in insubordination, rebellion, anti-authority or anti-company behavior, and resentment toward others.

## Anger/Ethics versus Compassion and Stability

One of the classic examples of a fatherless angry child is Kathy, who is fifty-four years old, single, and a stockbroker. She's no longer angry at her father or the world. She was born and raised on the Upper East Side of Manhattan. Her parents divorced when she was five years old. Kathy, starting from age five, saw her father only about once a year for lunch. She was allowed to meet him only at a certain restaurant and was never permitted to come to his house or office. She was allowed to call him only at his clothing company. Her father remarried when she was ten years old, and she has never even met her other three younger step-siblings from that marriage. According to Kathy, she didn't exist in her father's life after the divorce. She lost complete contact with her father when she was a teenager and has not spoken to him since (more than forty years ago). Kathy spent most of her twenties and thirties drinking heavily and numbing herself emotionally. She eventually discovered that her fatherlessness was her primary roadblock and driving her life into the ground. Her rage from being abandoned was propelling her life into constant fights at work, lost job opportunities, and relationship failures (divorced twice). She resolved her deep sense of rejection (see chapter 7) and began to be the woman that she wanted to be in her career, personal life, and her family. She even found compassion for her father and herself. This shift from anger to compassion allowed her to start developing a much more stable life and a far more productive career.

Today, Kathy is a recovering fatherless daughter. She moved to California twelve years ago to stop thinking and obsessing about her father's neglect in New York. She has shifted her attention, emotional energy, and angry thoughts, and that has caused her to become more compassionate and understanding of herself and others. Kathy marvels at her transformation concerning her father, her father factor, and herself. She is no longer stuck in the mire of hating her father or herself.

I sincerely doubt that you need much convincing, empirical evidence, or a list of true/false questions about whether or not you were a fatherless child. If this was your background, you know it. The problem that baffles so many fatherless adult children is how to cope with the early emotional devastation and despair that they experienced. Moreover, you may ask, how can you avoid those types of emotional situations that trigger anger at work? When you get emotionally hurt, the rage darts within you like a rushing river in springtime. There is no stopping the emotion or the damage done during these critical times. Yet all is not lost. Thinking about these issues becomes the groundwork for transforming your father factor.

But there are legitimate strengths that come from not having an active father figure in your life. Consider them and see what others you may have fostered.

## The Strengths of Children with Absent Fathers

- They understand the importance of saying no in the workplace.
- They have the emotional capacity to defuse and understand the tension that exists between coworkers.
- They are very faithful to those who show support, and they provide opportunities and professional support or approval.
- They have insight into how client, business, and work objectives need to be solved without being too emotionally attached to the outcome.
- They know the value and danger of expressing strong emotion in the workplace and in personal relationships.
- They are aware of the limited value of anger and rage in the workplace. Anger is a short-term solution to long-term problems in a career and life.
- They value hard work and stable business practices on a daily basis.
- They can be very objective, rational, and clear about how their career, their business, and their colleagues' careers should progress.
- They have leadership qualities because of their sense of fatherlessness—they are aware of the importance of supporting and lending approval to others.
- Coworkers like their demeanor of compassion and the ability to stand up for themselves and others.
- They know the rule book (they don't abandon their responsibilities) about being committed and consistent in the workplace and any relationship they're involved in.

We are all guilty at times of not focusing on the positive or thinking about the good values we received from our fathers while growing up. Unfortunately, it is usually after a death or some serious incident that our resentment shifts and we let go of those old wounds and painful misunderstandings. Regardless of how strained and painful the relationship was with your father, there is, in nearly every case, some degree of benefit and strength to be gleaned from it.

## FATHER FACTOR OF ACTION

Consider your approach in business and in life, and ask yourself, what are its strengths? Strengths listed or not listed are the foundation on which you want to build your new father factor. What strengths are missing from your career and life today? Every foundation has its core strength—what is yours?

Second, how can your natural roadblock, derived from your father, be obliterated from your life, your career, and your family? What steps do you need to take to rid yourself of it?

Third, what specific rules from your father contribute to one major hindrance in your career? How would you rewrite the rule for your current career situation?

Fourth, what is the father factor legacy that you want to impart to your coworkers, clients, immediate family, and to yourself? Consider what you want your legacy to be and how now to reinforce that theme in your job.

As we've seen, despite your relationship with your father, or, in some cases, because of it, you have acquired strengths that have served you well in life and in business. Let us see further how we can bolster those and add new strengths so you can reach your potential.

Chapter 11

# PUTTING YOUR CAREER IN THE FAST LANE
## The Next Level

One of the scariest things I have ever done is go beyond my father's career success and really become the person I have always wanted to be at work, at home, and with all the people in my life. It is still a little intimidating to have success and try to explain that to my father.

—Hank, age forty-seven

I barely knew my father growing up. He worked around the clock, and my parents were divorced. My mother and father were both hard workers in the local Ford factory. No one ever expected me to become a businesswoman and to create my own company. I never thought I would do it. I am so glad I did.

—Margaret, age thirty-nine

## WHO HOLDS THE KEYS?

One of your goals for reading this book is to take your career, your personal life, and your intimate and professional relationships to the next level of functioning. What is that level? The next level feels and looks like the following: there are more elements of fulfillment, and you reach your potential— (or get much closer to it), and everything, or most nearly everything, is working well for you. So the question of the day is, *what's your next level of growth and change in three areas of your life: professional, personal, and financial?*

By this point in our discussion you know that there is no way to get where you want to go without addressing your father's traits, habits, rules, and behaviors and their effect on you. We have discussed that all career paths run metaphorically through your father's house, which is the same one you lived in while growing up. *Your relationship with your father holds valuable information to unlocking both your personal success and professional empowerment.* This relationship can't be ignored. Your father-child issues can set you on the path to success—or sink your future. Adults face this fork in the road at some point in their personal and professional lives, marriages, friendships, and relationships and with their own children.

Your goal now is to get those keys (of information) from your father and unlock your future. There is nothing more empowering in people's lives than when they take full ownership, responsibility, and possession of their lives in all its various forms. The more information, insight, and knowledge you gather about your father-child relationship, the sooner you can take the keys and open up your future. One of the major premises to this entire book is: *You—not your father—hold the keys to your future.* If, for some reason, you aren't holding the keys, now is the time to get them in your hands. Think what it feels like when you hold the keys to your car, to your house, or to your office—there is an unconscious power, as well as an inner confidence, that goes with that mere possession. What gift do all sixteen-year-olds dream of and plead for their birthday? One guess, and it isn't clothes shopping or a paid trip to Hawaii; it is their very own car keys. That set of keys represents the ultimate in personal freedom and the next level in life. Adults crave that same freedom as much as any teenager does.

The same truth applies to your life and the evolution of your father factor. Nothing feels better than holding the keys to your own car, house, office, or hotel room on vacation; it just feels great. We all know the opposite effect when we lose our keys, and we can't find them anywhere in the house, in our purse, or in our desk. The sudden panic and rush of anxiety are the same deep feelings we carry when we don't know where our keys are to our future. What triggers even more panic is not having any idea of how to get our keys from our father or, in essence, how to become our own person and take control of our lives. These surges of panic are created in moments when we feel powerless in life, a feeling that none of us ever wants to experience. No one wants to feel helpless to change or move their life forward. This sense of personal and professional crisis happens when we aren't holding our keys!

We all know coworkers, colleagues, and friends in the workplace who will adamantly deny that their relationship with their father is a factor or contributes one way or another in their lives and careers. These adults tend to be the same people who don't consider the power (positively or negatively) that prior life experiences had in shaping who and what they are today. Thankfully for you, you know better. Now you fully know who needs to hold the keys to your next step: *you*. This acknowledgment allows you to pull all the different pieces of your father's influence together and move your entire life forward.

## HOW TO GET YOUR KEYS

Literature contains many stories about the power of taking your keys away from your father and the struggle that ensues. In order to stay on track, let's consider the idea of your getting your keys *without* fighting with your father. The compassionate-mentor father shows his children at a young age how their keys work—how to open their own doors and how to unlock their own treasures. This father has his own set of keys and knows the value of his children's having the same empowering experience. Sons and daughters of the C-M father enter adulthood the day that the emotional, mental, and psychological transaction takes place of their holding their own keys. The other four types of fathers aren't aware of the importance of showing their children how their keys work. In fact, many of these fathers hold on to them because they either don't trust their children completely or think it is not necessary for them to have so much freedom and personal power.

If we are going to take our keys back, then we have to consider the concept of forgiveness. According to an old wise saying, *The day you forgive your father is the day you enter adulthood.* Adulthood is all about owning and possessing your keys from your father. We discussed in chapter 7 about writing a letter to your father as a way of getting past your anger and resentment. There are as many ways to forgive as there are people in the world. The result of any degree of forgiveness is for you to find a way to let your father off the hook. This would be to forgive the emotional and mental debt that he has no way of ever repaying. Too many of our fathers probably owe us much more than we can write about or express to our closest friend. We can choose either to hold the grudge or to find a way to like ourselves better and release our fathers from our childhood pain and disappointment. Forgiveness helps the forgiver (you) to remove some of the old shame-based feelings of inadequacy and anger. Releasing your father elevates your emotional intelligence and mental aptitude. Another point is that by releasing your father, it allows you to no longer have one foot in the past and one in the present. This action puts all of your energy, emotions, and thoughts into the current-day events and structures of your life.

Forgiveness always benefits the giver much more than the receiver. Letting go of your internal demands, of wishes for being loved by your father, and of getting his approval are all dead weight in your emotional life, keeping you from progressing. That unresolved emotional weight carries right into your professional and personal relationships. Accepting who and what you are in your career, your relationships, and your family helps resolve the uncomfortable feelings of never feeling "good enough." Telling the most influential man in your life that you forgive him and have forgiven his debt is very empowering. Genuine forgiveness takes courage and compassion for yourself and your father.

Your quality of life will immediately improve by making this mental shift from demanding that your father pays up to writing off the debt— because he doesn't have the ability to ever repay you. *Your father is emotionally broke.* There is nothing you can do to fix your father. Your demanding repayment will only delay your personal development and personal growth. Most fathers, if they had the emotional means, would pay off the emotional debt to you and heal the wound. Regardless of your religious or nonreligious beliefs or spiritual orientation, forgiveness is a universal truth that is widely recognized as a life-changing event. The person who is changed for life is you! Remember that getting your keys from your father's hand is a transforming experience, but it takes forgiveness.

## PICTURE THIS EVENT

Imagine the following scene. You meet your father at your childhood home or at an exclusive restaurant, the beach, the mountains, or any place that feels safe for you to take possession of your keys. You know that your father is holding the one key that can open up your treasure chest that contains your talents, personal wealth, relationship fulfillment, and future success. When you see your father, you start the conversation with the most important words of your adult life: *Dad, I forgive you.* This conversation continues and takes longer than you thought or ever considered possible. While you are talking—saying what you would have always wanted to say to your father— you are amazed beyond belief that such an encounter would be possible. Even though your father may be dead, or you never met him or would never have this type of face-to-face discussion, still consider the validity of doing this powerful exercise. You begin to address the unresolved issues that have been nagging you for years. While you are talking, you notice that your feelings are under control, your thoughts are clear, and time is moving slowly. You are speaking from your heart in the most honest conversation that you have ever had with your father.

You lean forward and tell your father that you want the keys to your life and all the other things that have been locked by him. Your voice becomes tense, and your resentment is starting to show. Your father, in a moment of brilliance, says, "I don't have your keys. You have always had them—you just didn't know it." You pause and reply, "Then, who has the keys to my freedom, peace, and success?" Your father looks you straight in the eye and responds, "Forgiveness is your key to unlocking your life, and you have always had that power." You sit back, and you can't believe your ears and think your father is nuts. After pondering your father's comments, you agree that the approval, love, and acceptance were the doors *you* had to open in order to forgive him. Your act of forgiveness unlocks the other doors that you thought your father was responsible for keeping shut. The key that you have always wanted was always within your reach. *The key is forgiveness, and it started with forgiving your father.* You ask yourself, "Why didn't I do this sooner?" The only answer is you are now ready to open all the doors, talents, and treasures in your life. You thank your father for the gift of forgiveness, and you get up and leave. You realize, as you are walking away, that your life will never be the same after today's brief father-child encounter. Now you know how to change your life and bring your career and every other aspect of your life to the next level.

## DOING THE ACTUAL TALK

Your personal power, professional freedom, and drive to reach the next level feel well within your reach. This doesn't preclude your having to do hard work or juggling ten things at a time, including your other career—your family.

The following steps are designed for you to have this talk with your father. It isn't important to actually speak with him or even tell him about this interpersonal peace talk. *You are going to conduct this discussion facing a mirror and have it with yourself.* These tend to be the most powerful talks we ever have: **self-talk**.

1. Find a room with a mirror. Any type of room will do, but make sure it is private and big enough for you to walk around in.
2. Make a list of at least three things (no more than ten—otherwise it becomes overwhelming) that you need to discuss with your father that you have avoided for years. Don't be scared by the thought of his anticipated response or your own reluctance to bring up certain topics. The subject matter can range from your parents' chronic fighting, to your childhood verbal beatings, or to why your father has never said anything approving of you.
3. Stand or sit in front of the mirror and start with the only sentence you need: "Dad, I forgive you for . . ." Keep talking until there is no more emotion or energy left for your issues, concerns, topics, subjects, or feelings.
4. Don't use words like "always," "it's your fault," "never," "every time." Don't use name calling, finger pointing, blaming words, and so on. Express your feelings and thoughts without trying to verbally kill your father. You don't need to get in the last verbal dig with an aggressive word—the fight is over. Everyone wins. Stay away from blaming your father for all his shortcomings and screwups; it will only stall your transformation and change. Continuing to blame your father will not improve the quality of your life or career. Don't forget that your father is probably well aware of his shortcomings and screwups.
5. Now forgive *yourself* for holding these grudges, resentments, and disappointments. Accept the fact that you were not ready until today to move forward.
6. Thank your father for listening to you and for pointing out to you who really does hold the keys to your future: you!
7. After you do this exercise, make sure you debrief it, discuss it, and examine it with a friend, partner, or therapist.

This is a very intense exercise that can't be taken lightheartedly or passively. Forgiving your father for his past transgressions is a tremendous psychological step that most adults never take, usually avoid, and, most often, don't even consider. They just bury the pain and limp through life with a huge hole in their heart about their father-child relationship. The memory of their father is toxic to them and is dismissed as unimportant whenever it is mentioned or considered a life-changing influence. Their years of pain are too much to handle or to even speak about. No one has to keep living his adult life this way. The big key of forgiveness you now own is something that no one or any circumstance can ever take away from you. It is in your heart, mind, and thoughts. Your internal relationship with your father will never be the same because you have revised your father factor.

The key of forgiveness opens up the way to assemble all the pieces of your revised, amended, and reconstructed father factor. This step includes incorporating the elements of the compassionate-mentor fathering style into your life. Various experts from all fields of study (psychology, sociology, business, attachment behavior) consider the elements listed below as invaluable and as necessary as breathing for human development and healthy relationships. Being a C-M type of person, manager, partner, or parent is a very powerful force that will transform every area of your life and your relationships with the people around you.

## UNLOCKING YOUR INTERNAL ROADBLOCKS AND TRANSFORMING THEM INTO STRENGTHS

Your father-child relationship has elements of all ten of the positive variables listed in this chapter. Your father's legacy has given you strengths on which it is critical for you to continue to build. You are in the process of transforming the major roadblocks that each fathering style has into valuable strengths:

- shame into insight and understanding
- fear and avoidance into self-confidence and security
- low motivation and self-doubt into courage and strength of character
- anger into compassion and stability
- hopelessness and anxiety into leadership and vision

The combination of these various pieces of your new life, including for-giveness, makes up your transformed father factor. Through forgiveness and letting go of your resentments, you are beginning to transform shame into insight and understanding, fear and avoidance into self-confidence, low motivation and self-doubt into courage and strength of character, anger into compassion and stability and hopelessness into leadership and vision. Everyone has the same pieces and tools from their respective father-child relationships, but not everyone uses them or properly understands their value or purpose. The compassionate-mentor fathering style is the right balance, combination, and implementation of the strengths listed above. The C-M model allows for your individuality and personal touch in your career and all the different aspects of your life.

But how do you incorporate those values, behaviors, and skills into your life? For example, how do you stop operating as a superachiever daughter after doing it for all of your life? That question is very difficult to answer. The short answer is just to focus on these positive qualities listed above and stop doing the self-defeating things that derail your career momentum. The long answer is to change a few of your behaviors, amend your thoughts, and be aware of your career roadblocks. Both answers are correct, and both need to take place in your life.

Let's look at how to directly apply your C-M behaviors along with your particular strengths in your work world. Regardless of age, position, job expe-rience, rule-book conditions, education, and history with your father, you can work the ten C-M qualities into your life. Let's take a moment to remind our-selves that our life is more than our jobs, corporate position, income level, and power in the workplace. Your life is all these elements plus how you interact with your world: how you treat your family, children, friends, and others (phil-anthropic endeavors). These different parts plus your personal and professional relationship style compose the substance of your life.

The following list is the direct application of the C-M behaviors in the workplace as well as in everyday life. These qualities are the competitive edge that people are always searching for but rarely find in themselves and others. These talents, traits, and behaviors—the foundation to launch your career today—were popularized in the brilliant book sixty years ahead of its time titled *How to Win Friends and Influence People* by Dale Carnegie, who wrote about the value of friendships and how to treat and work with people in all facets of life. It is amazing that this book was written during the height of the Great Depression, when national unemployment rate was at 33 percent and when relationships weren't the first thought on people's minds in the workplace. Yet Carnegie knew that relationships matter more than money and more than the work pressures of his day. He was the first of many authors who recognized the immense value of being a compassionate person and a mentor to the people in one's personal and work life. It is this kind of timeless vision that has a long-lasting impact on people's lives and development. Carnegie had a compassionate-mentor father factor, and his message is still timeless seventy years later.[1]

## TEN COMPETITIVE C-M FACTORS FOR ALL CAREERS

The following list is a direct application of the ten qualities that you need to assimilate into your daily work behaviors, carpool discussions, morning briefings, business meetings, staff development discussions, team-building sessions, client dinners, sales meetings, and intimate discourse at night. These qualities are the cement that will become the foundation for any career path that you build. Second, there isn't a relationship or situation that you encounter during your day that will not require one of the following C-M styles and actions. Third, your goal is to blend your particular assets with these C-M traits, which will develop your personality and business strengths and keep your old limitations from holding you back.

Personality conflicts, personnel issues, and coworker misunderstandings are some of the silent problems that plague a company's productivity every day. These problems often manifest themselves in sick days, sick leave, or workman's compensation claims because of their frustrating nature for the individuals involved. Hardly anyone knows what to do with these conflicts, and for many it seems easier just to take a few days or weeks off from work and avoid the problem altogether. Very few people are equipped to handle the challenges of these sticky personnel ordeals.[2]

The actual work tends to be much easier than handling all the different relationship issues present in every work environment. Wherever you work, there are personality problems, "political issues," and human resource concerns because we are always dealing with people. It is part of the human experience, and it can't be avoided. That is why these C-M traits are so important to understand and carry with you into your world. The following list is designed to free your time from these common "no-win" personnel issues through the proactive measures of the C-M father factor.

*Tool #1—Allow flexibility, forgiveness, and compassion to influence your management style, coworker relationships, and client relations.* These three traits create an open line of communication between you and your listener. Any potentially explosive work situation is automatically defused with these three behavioral traits. The C-M factor is the application of insight and understanding versus shame and its paralyzing effect. Shame will always remove your capability to think clearly and make the best decisions. Shame blocks your emotional ability to be understanding, forgiving, and objective about any situation.

The application of the C-M father factor:

*Superachiever*—You don't insist on being right or having the final word on the matter. Don't focus on the need to be perfect and correct. You give up the role of being a know-it-all. You try to understand the other person's perspective.

*Time Bomb*—You don't overreact to a problem or a work setback. You allow for the fact that things don't always go according to your plan. You resist the temptation to yell or be aggressive toward your colleagues, supervisors, or employees. You are flexible and understanding with your coworkers' efforts and hard work.

*Passive*—You become mentally and emotionally engaged in the discussion or problem. You become part of the solution. You are emotionally aware of the issues concerning the particular question or people involved. You have insight into and understanding for your colleagues.

*Absent*—You don't avoid or dismiss a problem as nonsense. The subject or topic is of importance because it involves your colleagues or clients. You use your sense of flexibility to better understand why the topic or project is significant. You "show up" emotionally and mentally for your job.

***Tool #2***—*The ability to communicate in a clear and direct manner without the use of anger is of unlimited personal and professional value to you.* Your feelings toward others (compassion and empathy) are to be used as information and can be very helpful in understanding a personnel, client, or business situation. You have learned to trust your instincts, feelings, and inner thoughts about people, decisions, and relationships. You are increasingly aware of the "human" factor at work and with the people you deal with every day.

The application of the C-M father factor to communication:

*Superachiever*—You allow yourself to view your colleagues as people with their own opinions. You view people as more than performance cogs in the workplace. You have compassion for your coworkers, which creates stability for you and your career. Their opinions need to be heard and understood by you. You will likely learn something.

*Time Bomb*—You resist the temptation to yell or to communicate in a condescending way. You respect the rights and thoughts of others as a way of controlling your anger and frustration.

*Passive*—You engage the feelings and thoughts of your coworkers. You start forming stronger work attachments and relationships with the people surrounding your career. You start to show compassion and emotional stability in all your relationships.

*Absent*—You are aware of the basic emotional needs of all people for love, support, and approval. You have these three qualities active in your interactions with people in all areas of your life. These three emotional C-M factors are exhibited in your behavior by being compassionate and empathic at work and at home with your family.

***Tool #3***—*Relationships matter!* Your ability to connect to, understand, and empathize with others will automatically move your career forward. You have the self-confidence and security in your career to be a team member in the workplace. Your embracing of the C-M model places relationships as the number one priority in your career. You know the long-lasting value of nurturing people's needs and their sense of belonging. This mental shift allows you to be a mentor and leader to all those you support emotionally and mentally.

In applying the C-M model to your work relationships, the *super-achiever, time-bomb, passive*, and *absent* styles will all evolve a greater understanding of people's need for positive, stable, and consistent relationships regardless of age, gender, position, and wealth. You will have a deeper respect for the human element within you instead of only the business element. Your coworkers will respect you and your commitment to them and their careers. People will be much more willing and able to help you develop your career and life. Your support of others will show in your self-confidence to develop relationships with all the people surrounding your life as well.

*Tool #4—You become aware that everyone in the workplace, and in life, has a "father factor" dynamic.* You understand and value the influence that your father factor had on you, and you have developed and amended it. You can now truly understand the office politics at work because of the underlying influence that everyone's fathers had on their lives. You have insight, wisdom, and practical advice on how to transform your colleagues' "father factor" roadblocks in their personal and professional lives. Your experience with relating to your father naturally allows you to be a mentor to the men and women involved in your life—without becoming preachy. Mentoring is always based on life experience and foresight, both of which you have to offer to your family, friends, and coworkers. You will have a working knowledge of the different fathering styles and how they play themselves out in relationships in all areas of your life.

The application of the mentor role in your transformed C-M father factor:

*Superachiever*—You allow people the room and experience to grow and learn from their mistakes and challenges. You offer support and approval, regardless of the outcome or result. You embrace being a mentor rather than focusing only on results, outcomes, and bottom-line profits. People's self-worth is more meaningful to you than their appearance.

*Time Bomb*—You understand people's need to develop a sense of competence and self-worth through achievement. You aren't critical or demanding that the results can be only a certain way. You give up your need to control everything. You don't resist or try to control other peoples' father factors at work. You lend support when asked.

*Passive*—You are aware that everyone at work and in your life needs support to develop and change. You aren't emotionally distant or unavailable to be a mentor to colleagues and friends.

*Absent*—You understand the importance of being a mentor to your family, friends, and colleagues. You are present and active with the people in your relationships. The sense of rage for never having a father/leader is resolved. You have become the kind of mentor that you have always wanted.

**Tool #5**—*Career strengths and weaknesses can be better understood by knowing a person's rule book and how it operates.* Having the insight and Understanding that everyone is guided by his father's spoken and unspoken rules is a tremendous tool. Appreciating that why someone does what is based on his father's rule book is invaluable for any relationship. This degree of insight, understanding, perception, and appreciation for the struggles that people go through to rewrite their own rule book is priceless. This allows C-M managers to develop the potential of those around them and removes the element of shame and self-doubt from others.

The application of C-M father factor to a new sense of understanding:

*Superachiever*—You appreciate the emotional struggles that people have for separating from their fathers' unspoken rule book. You understand that a person's value is more than his achievements, position, wealth, or accomplishments. It is becoming his own person as a positive force in the workplace and in his personal life that really counts.

*Time Bomb*—Patience, patience, patience is your gift to the people in your life and their struggles with their rule books. You have the insight to understand that it isn't important for people to do what you think they should. You know that people many times don't know the deep psychological impact of their fathers' rule book on their adult behavior.

*Passive*—You actively support the people in your career by quietly helping them rewrite their rule book and helping them move to their next career level—without your proselytizing. You know your emotional commitment is critical to your coworkers, family, and friends. Your involvement is a very powerful force and helps spark positive change in the people who are a part of your life.

*Absent*—No one can succeed if she refuses to be actively involved in the lives of the people who are part of her career and personal life. You resist the temptation to be aloof and removed from the needs of your colleagues. You understand the importance of assisting willing candidates in rewriting their rule books and following their new rules.

**Tool #6**—*Adults, coworkers, partners, family members, and supervisors always respond positively to the C-M model.* You actively embrace the ten strengths of the C-M model in your career and life. You know that, if your career or personal life is going to move forward, these elements will do it. There is no internal argument or emotional roadblock to being the professional you have always wanted to be. You know that whatever your emotional or psychological roadblock is, the C-M style will resolve it.

The application of the C-M father factor with strength and security:

*Superachiever*—You no longer hold onto the outdated belief that the only measure of a person is his professional status. You know that there is much more to a person's life than just achievement and outward appearance.

*Time Bomb*—You allow yourself to become the person, partner, parent, and professional you always wanted as a child: patient, compassionate, understanding, secure, and strong. You develop the emotional strength to tolerate differences and contrary opinions.

*Passive*—You don't allow yourself to fall into the old, familiar rut of being on the periphery of your career, personal life, and relationships. You apply the strengths of the C-M factor and are actively involved in all areas of your life. You don't dismiss people's emotional needs and concerns as irrelevant.

*Absent*—You know the emotional damage created by your prior exodus from your professional and personal responsibilities. You actively apply the C-M strengths and avoid the disasters of abandoning people in your life.

***Tool #7***—*Through the C-M model, you reach a balance of assertiveness between the extremes of aggressiveness and passivity.* All children learn, as a result of their father-child relationship, to be either aggressive or passive in the workplace. The best balance to these two extremes is the middle pathway of being assertive and courageous. Assertiveness is the ability to express your desires, wishes, and/or opinions in a firm, constructive manner. The C-M manager can be assertive without isolating or alienating her employees or colleagues.

The application of the C-M model to areas of courage and security:

*Superachiever*—You are learning that overpowering people or forcing your opinion is the least productive way of attaining your desired results. Your use of courage and security in the form of assertiveness is appropriate in the workplace.

*Time Bomb*—You know that people respond better to your assertive decisions. People respect your courage and emotional security in presenting your requests in a positive, assertive manner but not in a belligerent manner.

*Passive*—You have opinions, wishes, and visions that you feel strongly about. You are learning that being assertive is your best communication tool in all areas of your life. You no longer ignore your thoughts and feelings and those of others.

*Absent*—You are becoming emotionally engaged with all areas of your career and life. The balanced approach of being assertive with people requires you to interact consistently and to be connected. Your active presence takes courage and security in your career.

***Tool #8***—*You don't seek the approval of others in your decisions or actions.* You have the emotional insight and understanding that approval-seeking behavior always weakens your career development and how you feel about yourself. The C-M employee knows that approval seeking is a vicious cycle of feeling powerless and insecure. You have developed a healthy sense of what your emotional, personal, and occupational wants are and how to fulfill them. Working in this positive way, you don't need validation.

The application of the C-M model of insight and understanding in terms of approval:

> *Superachiever*—You have learned that giving your support and approval to others' efforts is a very positive force (though you are not dependent on these behaviors yourself). These types of supportive behaviors can change the direction of others' lives and boost their career development in a forward motion.

> *Time Bomb*—The use of affirming statements, insight, and supportive actions will transform the people in your life. Your positive approach to people in your career and life will help create a productive work environment.

> *Passive*—Your active verbal and nonverbal support of your coworkers creates a foundation for growth and change. You understand the power of being positive and supportive of others. This C-M style transforms your career into a powerful force with unlimited potential.

> *Absent*—You know and apply the psychological insight that all people, regardless of age or career status, have—the basic need for love and support (approval). You know this C-M truth and apply it in your career and personal life.

***Tool #9***—*You know that a person's sense of competence and personal drive are first established in the father-child relationship.* This understanding is critical in seeing coworkers not in a vacuum, but more fully in the context of their development. The C-M adult knows that a person's actions, motivation, career drive, and self-confidence are connected to the fathering style with which he was raised. The compassionate view of people allows you to comprehend more completely all the different variables that go into making a person's life and career. You suspend making judgments of your coworkers and focus instead on learning more about them in a positive way.

The application of compassion and stability through the C-M model: Those with *superachiever, time-bomb, passive,* and *absent* father factors all have the potential to see others in the context of their own father factor. This insight explains the different motivations, drives, rules, and beliefs that people have in the workplace, and a comprehensive view of why and how people operate in their daily life is strategic for advancing your own career growth. Without this compassionate, mentoring view of people, your influence and potential in your career would be greatly reduced. How people function in their careers is a complex issue—the personal drive, competence to excel, and sense of well-being start in a person's father-child relationship and continues thereon. The more you know about that dynamic, the more you can be a mentoring influence in the lives of your coworkers.

*Tool #10—People in all levels of a corporation, business community, or any work setting need the same three elements in their lives: support, empathy, and approval.* The C-M person knows the value of these three core values that are the foundation in an adult's life. People will spend their entire lives seeking out these three elements. Fathers provide these elements in varying degrees based on their attachment style, fathering style, and rule book guidelines. The C-M person, regardless of gender, can be the good father figure that most adults never experienced growing up. If you had a C-M father, then you know firsthand the intrinsic value of being that type of manager or coworker and friend to others. The C-M person brings a positive force to everyone's life and circumstances. People will follow the C-M person because of his excellent people skills and knowledge. Every child craves to be loved, supported, and understood, so why would adults be any different? The obvious answer is that we all are the same, and these values are timeless. Though the C-M manager would appreciate receiving this kind of nurturing from his supervisors, he does not depend on it, and he knows that his value is from within.

The application of Tool #10 is the summary of the success formula of your newly transformed father factor. There is nothing in your life that will not immediately benefit from the implementation of these core values. Your career will soar much higher through this approach, and your relationships will deepen with people in every facet of your life.

Chapter 12

# GOING BEYOND YOUR FATHER
## Putting It All Together

My father told me what specialty of medicine to choose. I knew it was a wrong choice for me at the time. He wanted me to be a general surgeon. I knew my calling was to be a pediatrician and deliver babies. I am so glad that I didn't listen to my father on that issue.

—Allison, age forty-four

I was sitting in a restaurant today, and I wrote down all the ways I am like my father. It is amazing how passive and noncommittal I am with work and relationships. I am just like my father. I have to become more active and not fear commitment; it's my pattern.

—Lonnie, age forty-three

Imagine you are sitting in your office on a Wednesday afternoon, feeling relaxed and accomplished, or at a client business meeting, making a PowerPoint presentation, and you have a sense of relief and a deep confidence in what you are doing. You don't carry any of the weight of the seven father factor roadblocks in your life any longer. There are no negative side effects of your father's legacy operating in your business or personal life. You function at your full capacity professionally with the C-M talents and strengths you've been honing. You use all your resources and personal power in the workplace. This isn't a dream! This is—or will be—your life. The timeless question that is asked when people are presented with this career picture is: But how does this happen?

*The answers are on every page of this book: **you**.* You are the answer and, if you choose, also the problem. Most adults hear that answer and reflexively wonder how can they go from point A to point B without repeating past disappointments, habitual frustrations, and endless career moves leading nowhere. The difference is you. Since you have uncovered the unseen roadblocks, fixed the broken pipes, and changed the rules, your life is now moving in the direction you want. Those three variables alone will improve any person's career opportunities regardless of his past or present failures. Now you are entering a phase in your life with the type of personal fulfillment and empowerment that you have only dreamed about. You are no longer going to look at colleagues and friends and wonder why things don't go your way. Now is your time to move forward. The tools are all there for you to use and adjust to your particular work situation.

The importance of your relationship with your father is something that will evolve throughout your life. The developing of deeper self-discovery and growth is an ongoing process for which there isn't a stopping point. The key is to remember that, no matter what has happened or has not happened, your personal and professional lives need to progress. At the end of the day, there is no substitution for action. You have all the tools, insight, and forgiveness necessary to move forward in your life.

## FATHER FACTOR CHANGE—NOW IS THE TIME

After all, what is your father factor? It is the conscious understanding and awareness of the significant role that your father had in forming your career path, professional behavior, and professional and personal relationships. This understanding affects not just your career but every aspect of your life, including your love life, partner selection, parenting skills, and body image. There isn't an area of your life, in fact, that hasn't been touched by your father's influence. Regardless of the quality of your father-child relationship while growing up, you have a huge benefit from that relationship. The more you learn about that benefit, the better your life will be.

As you well know by this point in our discussion, there are primarily five styles of fathering, each with its own strengths and weaknesses. The most productive fathering style, the compassionate-mentor, is the model of the ideal manager, empowered employee, and self-motivated businessperson, and these people reflect this style of relating and being. This powerful approach is the healthiest father factor and will put your career in the fast lane. The eight strengths of the C-M are the keys that may be used repeatedly to unlock your potential on a personal and professional level. You can call these strengths anything you want, but they need to be part of your everyday professional toolbox.

## Your Father Factor Strengths

- Insight and Understanding
- Self-Confidence and Security
- Courage and Strength of Character
- Compassion and Stability

Remember to draw on these strengths every day at work and with your family and loved ones.

You have nearly finished reading this book and know that change is in your immediate future. You know what your roadblocks are (e.g., shame, fear or avoidance, lack of motivation, self-doubt, anger and no ethical responsibility), and you want to propel your life forward. In fact, you have resolved to make these changes today. The previous eleven chapters have been chock-full of ideas, suggestions, and pleas for amending your professional behavior. The various details of overcoming the roadblocks in your own style have been addressed repeatedly in each chapter.

Unlocking the door to your future is all in your hands. You have the power to achieve, regardless of your past beliefs and rules. One of the scariest parts of being an adult is that we are absolutely, 100 percent responsible for our lives and the choices we make. *Our father isn't even remotely responsible for our life now—it's all ours!* Your father is clearly a major influence in your life, but it isn't his life. One of the foundations of this book is that the father blame game is over and no longer an option. In fact, you probably can't tolerate your friends or coworkers doing their father bashing any longer. There is no purpose in trying to kill the horrible feelings that we feel about our father. The only way out of the father rut is to overhaul your father factor and all the different elements connected to it. The key to unlocking your future is to let your father off the hook. As stated earlier, your father doesn't have the emotional means to pay off the debt he owes you. It is your bill, and you now know how to wipe it off your books. Allow yourself the freedom to not carry around this debt that no one is capable of canceling other than you.

These seven steps are the pragmatic, linear plan to move mountains in your career. There is nothing that you can't accomplish with this direct, fundamental plan.

## The Seven Steps to Success

**1. Make a commitment to change.** There is an old, wise saying in psychology: "You are only as strong as your weakest commitment." If there is one thing you can do that will alter the course of your career and life, it is simply making a commitment to change. Your commitment will be the glue that will get you through the difficult times of anxiety, uncertainty, and fear. You know what your career weaknesses are and why they need to change. You also know how these behaviors, rules, and attachments are connected to your style.

Right now, identify five goals for your career and personal life. Think big. Second, set a realistic timetable for each of these goals to be accomplished. Write down how these goals can be achieved and measured. Third, list the behaviors that realistically sabotage your progression in your career and in relationships. If you are having problems doing this step, ask your partner, a close friend, or a trustworthy colleague. They, too, know about your strengths and weaknesses.

**2. Improve your self-awareness.** Keep a journal of emotions. Writing down your reactions forces you to stop and become aware of your unconscious feelings and thoughts. This will help you keep track of your sabotaging yourself with critical thoughts and negative feelings. Carefully chronicle pertinent work situations that you want to change, including both good and bad encounters, feelings, and general things you've wanted to do. Take a few minutes to write down how you want to handle a certain situation next time. This practice will reveal over time a more positive way of handling problematic issues. Slowly, you will retrain your automatic thoughts, responses, and actions to take a more compassionate-mentor approach to dealing with the situation. You will reinforce the new insight of consciously creating new, more productive professional and personal behavior patterns. Writing down your reactions forces you to stop and become aware of your unconscious thoughts and feelings.

This journal can also be used for rewriting your father's rule book (see chapter 9), which is part and parcel to increasing your self-awareness. Your father's unspoken rules are often the stumbling blocks to your forward motion. The more you know about these rules, the quicker you can write your own rule book for living your life.

**3. Identify your triggers.** List ten things that always set you off like an unguided missile. Knowing what your hot spots are at work, at home, and in your relationships will dramatically reduce your anger and frustration. If you know, for instance, that certain behaviors, such as a nonanswer to a direct question, upset you, then you can plan ahead of time for a different response.

Over time you will not only change your behavior but also find that the people in your life will respond to you differently. Don't underestimate the impact that your changed behavior will have on how people think of and relate to you. By pinpointing your own triggers, you will be more aware of how to reduce your angry, self-destructive behavior and feelings. This list is very important because you are taking responsibility, control, and preventive action about your shaming behaviors. Losing your patience leaves you wide open to negative, self-destructive feelings and thoughts. The critical father in all our heads uses these types of situations to condemn, frustrate, and stall our progression. Use your new father factor insight and knowledge to help you anticipate future events and how to successfully defuse them.

**4. Don't allow your mistakes or career setbacks to derail your commitment to change.** What will you do when a hot spot pops up in your future? The learning curve is the steepest in the first few weeks of any type of behavioral modification. Frustrating things are going to happen, generally more often in the beginning of your new program. The answer is to develop a plan ahead of time for defusing potentially problematic situations. The more prepared you are for the unexpected or the unusual problem, the quicker you can resume your new course of action and functioning. The change in your father factor is all about reacting to the old work situations with a new perspective and approach.

For instance, when you feel yourself losing your temper or getting frustrated, take a three-minute time-out. Always think in terms of changing your physical circumstances in a pressured situation. The physical change allows our "fight-or-flight" response to stop functioning, and we can regain our cognitive control. Another idea is get a drink of water and break the emotional cycle in your mind and thoughts. The psychology behind your taking "time out" is that it allows you to act and think more consciously and deliberately. It also short-circuits the old response cycle in your mind and keeps you from getting swept away with your anger. Post your plan somewhere so you will see it frequently during the day—for example, on your computer. The goal is to imprint your new C-M father factor style on your mind.

**5. Be aware of old, familiar father factor habits.** You are only human, so try to be compassionate with yourself. Things will go wrong on occasion, given your triggers from the list above. This step is more about your unconscious habits that stop your career from moving forward. For instance, if your issue is always pleasing people, seeking approval, or feeling a lack of confidence, then make a plan that will address these behaviors when they might occur. There are work situations that cause you to slip into these self-defeating behaviors, so take time to identify them ahead of time. These preventive plans are critical for change. On one side of a sheet of paper, make a list of the major father factor habits that cause you the greatest problems, difficulty, frustration, and emotional pain. This list is the key to moving your career path to the next level of functioning. On the other half of that page, make a list of your career strengths. Look at the contrast. Don't dismiss your strengths because your approach has been passive and you want to be more of a C-M person. You are adding tools to your already-existing talents and strengths every day.

You know what predominant fathering style you were raised with and its inherent strengths and weaknesses. Be aware of what sets your career spinning forward and what sends it spiraling backwards. The chapter that describes your father factor and its strengths are tools for your improvement. When you feel yourself starting to revert to your old patterns, catch them before they escalate. Your recovery plan can be as simple as not to say yes every time you feel uncomfortable or insecure. Another example is not to become verbally aggressive or belligerent when you feel hurt or threatened by your coworkers or clients. When those feelings arise in you, your plan is to become assertive and express your feelings to the best of your ability, but in a calm and clear manner.

**6. Get a support system in place.** There is no way you can go about this process without support. This is one step where so many people drop the ball. For whatever the reason, adults are typically embarrassed to expose their needs to other adults. It is mind-boggling that people will do all this internal work to change their father factor and move their career to the next level but refuse to let anyone know about it. If this a sticking point for you, this issue needs to be addressed. If you can't share your life dreams and goals with someone else, that is a serious roadblock to furthering your professional and personal life. Allowing people to be emotionally close to you is a C-M trait and a great resource for your future.

Your chances of continued success will be much more attainable with emotional and psychological support. Find a friend, spouse, or mentor with whom you can openly discuss your father factor plan, preferably a loyal friend in the workplace. Let your supporter and/or support system know what your objectives are and how you are going to accomplish them. Your support system can help hold you accountable and encourage you. If you find that you need even more support in overcoming your roadblocks, then consider the assistance of a psychologist.

**7. Determine what success looks like and set your goals for achieving it.** How can you hold yourself accountable, know you are changing, or move forward if there's no yardstick to measure your progress? Create an evaluation timetable for your goals and stick to it as closely as possible. Your support system should also know about this measuring tool. For instance, you can keep track of how many times you become angry in a week. Then, try to reduce it by 50 percent over the following two weeks. Perhaps you will review your progress with your close friend(s) every two months and get feedback. You can always ask your partner for insight on progress and change. The people we live with tend to help us see the whole story, whether or not we like it. Over time, you will soon discover that your new father factor approach—as shown in your new consciously created behaviors—is starting to become a habit.

Knowing what success looks and feels like for you is one of the quickest ways to move your career forward. Everyone has his or her own idea of what personal and professional success looks and feels like. Don't limit yourself to considering merely economic gains as the only measurement of success. Success comes in many forms, through different events and types of evolving relationships.

## SUMMARY

I want to leave you with one of my favorite quotes. There is nothing that takes the place of:

Persistence

> Nothing in the world can take the place of persistence. Talent will not; nothing is more common than unsuccessful men with talent. Genius will not; unrewarded genius is almost a proverb. Education will not; the world is full of educated derelicts. Persistence and determination alone are omnipotent.
>
> —Calvin Coolidge

This wonderful quote by Calvin Coolidge is priceless, timeless, and very true.[1] There is nothing you are going to do in your career that will not require your persistence and determination. The pillars of your revised father factor will have these two traits some place in the foundation or on the ground floor. Regardless of your education, talents, strengths, perceived insecurities, or traumatic, painful father-child relationship, achievement is possible only with persistence. The world responds well to persistence; it almost always prevails.

I have found that anyone who applies the seven steps to success above and combines them with an expanded understanding of his father factor—plus determination and persistence—not only will exceed his goals but also find his place in life. There are so many ways to move your life, career, relationships, and finances forward, and they are all tied to your persistence and determination. You wouldn't be reading this last page if it wasn't in you to move your life forward. You now have a deeper understanding of the issues that have plagued your life and how to overcome them. What I can't give you is the persistence necessary to finish this project called your life. That "it" is inside of you, and only you can make things happen. You now have all the keys, knowledge, insight, and courage to make the changes you have always wanted.

Last, whatever you do, *do* something. Don't allow a failed marriage, a broken business relationship, a personnel clash, a bankruptcy, a criminal arrest, poor career choices, or being fired hold you back anymore. It's your time to move forward. Life is full of people who have given up and can intelligently argue that you should do the same. If you don't act in your best interest and concern, there aren't enough drugs to take away the sense of regret and depression you will face. I urge you to reconsider your life and keep moving forward. Remember, there is no longer any substitution for action. You have the keys. Once you have the keys, you can open all the doors you want.

# ENDNOTES

## CHAPTER 2

1. John Bowlby, *A Secure Base: Parent-Child Attachment and Healthy Human Development* (New York: Basic Books, 1988), pp. 89–99.
2. John Bowlby, *Attachment and Loss* (New York: Basic Books, 1969), pp. 156–75.

## CHAPTER 4

1. Jane Middelton-Moz, *Shame and Guilt: The Masters of Disguise* (Deerfield Beach, FL: Health Communications, 1990), pp. 8–34.

## CHAPTER 5

1. Edmund Bourne and Lorna Garano, *Coping with Anxiety: 10 Simple Ways to Relieve Anxiety, Fear and Worry* (Oakland, CA: New Harbinger, 2003), pp. 76–99.
2. Edmund Bourne, Arlen Brownstein, and Lorna Garano, *Natural Relief for Anxiety* (Oakland, CA: New Harbinger, 2004), pp. 155–79.
3. Rex Briggs, *Transforming Anxiety, Transcending Shame* (Deerfield Beach, FL: Health Communications, 1999), pp. 81–89.
4. Albert Ellis, *A Guide to Rational Living*, 3rd ed. (North Hollywood, CA: Wilshire, 1998), chaps. 1–3.

## CHAPTER 6

1. John C. Masters, Thomas G. Burish, and David C. Rimm, *Behavior Therapy: Techniques and Empirical Findings*, 3rd ed. (San Diego: Harcourt Brace Jovanovich, 1987), chap. 6.

## CHAPTER 7

1. Stephan B. Poulter, *Father Your Son: How to Become the Father You Have Always Wanted to Be* (New York: McGraw-Hill, 2004), appendix 2.

2. Ricci Isolina, *Mom's House, Dad's House—A Complete Guide for Parents Who Are Separated, Divorced, or Remarried* (New York: Fireside, 1997), pp. 88–94.

## CHAPTER 11

1. Dale Carnegie, *How to Win Friends and Influence People* (New York: Simon & Schuster, 1936), pp. 12–25.

2. Dale Carnegie, *How to Stop Worrying and Start Living: Time-Tested Methods for Conquering Worry* (New York: Simon & Schuster, 1944), pp. 99–111.

## CHAPTER 12

1. Wayne W. Dyer, *Wisdom of the Ages: A Modern Master Brings Eternal Truths into Everyday Life* (New York: HarperCollins, 2002), pp. 78–87.

# BIBLIOGRAPHY

Amen, Daniel G., and Routh, Lisa C. *Healing Anxiety and Depression*. New York: Putnam, 2003.

Anderson, Nancy. *Work with Passion: How to Do What You Love for a Living*. Novato, CA: New World Library, 2004.

Biddulph, Steve. *Raising Boys: Why Boys Are Different—And How to Help Them Become Happy and Well-Balanced Men*. Berkeley, CA: Celestial Arts, 1998.

Bly, Robert. *Iron John: A Book about Men*. Reading, MA: Addison-Wesley, 1990.

Bourne, Edmund J., Arlen Brownstein, and Lorna Garano. *Natural Relief for Anxiety*. Oakland, CA: New Harbinger, 2004.

Bourne, Edmund, and Lorna Garano. *Coping with Anxiety: 10 Simple Ways to Relieve Anxiety, Fear and Worry*. Oakland, CA: New Harbinger, 2003.

Bowlby, John. *Attachment and Loss*. New York: Basic Books, 1969.

———. *A Secure Base: Parent-Child Attachment and Healthy Human Development*. New York: Basic Books, 1988.

Bray, James H., and John Kelly. *Stepfamilies: Love, Marriage, and Parenting in the First Decade*. New York: Broadway Books, 1998.

Brazelton, T. Berry. *Working & Caring*. Reading, MA: Addison-Wesley, 1992.

Briggs, Rex. *Transforming Anxiety, Transcending Shame*. Deerfield Beach, FL: Health Communications, 1999.

Brott, Armin A. *Father for Life: A Journey of Joy, Challenge, and Change*. New York: Abbeville Press, 2003.

Brown, Byron. *Soul without Shame: A Guide to Liberating Yourself from the Judge Within*. Boston: Shambhala Publications, 1999.

Canada, Geoffrey. *Reaching up for Manhood: Transforming the Lives of Boys in America*. Boston: Beacon Press, 1998.

Carnegie, Dale. *How to Win Friends and Influence People.* New York: Simon & Schuster, 1936.

———. *How to Stop Worrying and Start Living: Time-Tested Methods for Conquering Worry.* New York: Simon & Schuster, 1944.

Covey, Stephen R. *The Seven Habits of Highly Effective Families.* New York: Golden Books, 1997.

Dacey, John S., and Lisa B. Fiore. *Your Anxious Child. How Parents and Teachers Can Relieve Anxiety in Children.* San Francisco: Jossey-Bass, 2002.

Davidson, Jonathan, and Henry Dreher. *The Anxiety Book: Developing Strength in the Face of Fear.* New York: Riverhead Books, 2003.

Dayton, Tian. *The Magic of Forgiveness: Emotional Freedom and Transformation at Midlife.* Deerfield Beach, FL: Health Communications, 2003.

Deak, JoAnn, with Teresa Barker. *Girls Will Be Girls. Raising Confident and Courageous Daughters.* New York: Hyperion, 2002.

Deida, David. *The Way of the Superior Man: A Spiritual Guide to Mastering the Challenges of Work, Women, and Sexual Desire.* Austin, TX: Plexus, 1997.

DeRosis, Helen. *Women & Anxiety: A Step-by-Step Program for Managing Anxiety and Depression.* New York: Hatherleigh Press, 1998.

Dobson, James C. *New Hide or Seek.* Grand Rapids, MI: Fleming H. Revell, 1999.

Drucker, Peter F., with Joseph A. Maciariello. *The Daily Drucker: 366 Days of Insight and Motivation for Getting the Right Things Done.* New York: HarperBusiness, 2004.

Dumaine, Deborah. *Write to the Top: Writing for Corporate Success,* 3rd ed. New York: Random House Trade Paperback Edition, 2004.

Dyer, Wayne W. *There's a Spiritual Solution to Every Problem.* New York: HarperCollins, 2001.

———. *Wisdom of the Ages: A Modern Master Brings Eternal Truths into Everyday Life.* New York: HarperCollins, 2002.

Eliot, John. *Overachievement: The New Model for Exceptional Performance.* New York: Portfolio, 2004.

Ellis, Albert. *A Guide to Rational Living,* 3rd ed. North Hollywood, CA: Wilshire, 1988.

Estes, Clarissa P. *Women Who Run with the Wolves.* New York: Ballantine Books, 1992.

Farber, Steve. *The Radical Leap: A Personal Lesson in Extreme Leadership.* Chicago: Dearborn Trade, 2004.

Gallo, E., and Jon Gallo. *Silver Spoon Kids: How Successful Parents Raise Responsible Children.* New York: McGraw-Hill, 2001.

———. *The Financially Intelligent Parent: Eight Steps to Raising Emotionally Aware and Financially Responsible Children.* New York: Penguin Books, 2005.

Garbarino, James, and Ellen deLara. *And Words Can Hurt Forever: How to Protect Adolescents from Bullying, Harassment, and Emotional Violence.* New York: Free Press, 2002.

———. *Parents under Siege: Why You Are the Solution, Not the Problem, in Your Child's Life.* Carmichael, CA: Touchstone Books, 2002.

———. *Raising Children in a Socially Toxic Environment.* San Francisco: Jossey-Bass, 1995.

Gilligan, James. *Violence: Our Deadly Epidemic and Its Causes.* New York: Putnam, 1996.

Gottman, John. *Raising an Emotionally Intelligent Child.* New York: Simon & Schuster, 1997.

Gurian, Michael. *A Fine Young Man: What Parents, Mentors, and Educators Can Do to Shape Adolescent Boys into Exceptional Men.* New York: Jeremy P. Tarcher, 1999.

———. *The Soul of the Child: Nurturing the Divine Identity of Our Children.* New York: Atria Books, 2002.

———. *The Wonder of Boys. What Parents, Mentors and Educators Can Do to Shape Young Boys into Exceptional Men.* New York: Putnam, 1996.

Harris, Judith Rich. *The Nurture Assumption: Why Children Turn Out the Way They Do.* New York: Free Press, 1998.

Harrison, Harry H., Jr. *Father to Daughter: Life Lessons on Raising a Girl.* New York: Workman Publishing, 2003.

Johnsgard, Keith. *Conquering Depression and Anxiety through Exercise.* Amherst, NY: Prometheus Books, 2004.

Judson, Bruce. *Go It Alone: The Secret to Building a Successful Business on Your Own.* New York: HarperCollins, 2004.

Kelly, Joe. *Dads and Daughters. How to Inspire, Understand, and Support Your Daughter When She's Growing up So Fast.* New York: Broadway Books, 2005.

Kimmel, Michael. *Manhood in America: A Cultural History.* New York: Free Press, 1996.

Kindlon, Dan. *Too Much of a Good Thing: Raising Children of Character in an Indulgent Age.* New York: Hyperion, 2001.

Lang, Gregory E. *Why a Daughter Needs a Dad: 100 Reasons.* Nashville, TN: Cumberland House, 2002.

Lansky, Vicky. *101 Ways To Be a Special Dad.* Chicago: Contemporary Books, 1993.

LaRossa, Ralph. *The Modernization of Fatherhood: A Social and Political History.* Chicago: University of Chicago Press, 1997.

Leman, Kevin. *What a Difference a Daddy Makes.* Nashville, TN: Thomas Nelson, 2000.

Levine, Mel. *Ready or Not, Here Life Comes.* New York: Simon & Schuster, 2005.

Levine, Suzanne B. *Father Courage: What Happens When Men Put Family First.* New York: Harcourt, 2000.

Loeber, Rolf, and David P. Farrington. *Serious and Violent Juvenile Offenders: Risk Factors and Successful Interventions.* Thousand Oaks, CA: Sage, 1998.

Lofas, Jeannette, and Dawn B. Sova. *Stepparenting.* New York: Zebra Books, 1985.

Mac Kenzie, Robert J. *Setting Limits: How to Raise Responsible, Independent Children by Providing Reasonable Boundaries.* Rocklin, CA: Prima Publishing, 1993.

Masters, John C., Thomas G. Burish, and David C. Rimm. *Behavior Therapy: Techniques and Empirical Findings,* 3rd ed. San Diego: Harcourt Brace Jovanovich, 1987.

Maxwell, John C. *Winning with People: Discover the People Principles that Work for You Every Time.* Nashville, TN: Nelson Books, 2004.

Middelton-Moz, Jane. *Shame and Guilt: The Masters of Disguise.* Deerfield Beach, FL: Health Communications, 1990.

Moore, Thomas. *Care of the Soul.* New York: HarperCollins, 1992.

O'Connell, Mark. *The Good Father: On Men, Masculinity, and Life in the Family.* New York: Scribner, 2005.

Oh, Kara. *Men Made Easy. How To Get What You Want From Your Man.* Beverly Hills, CA: Avambre Press, 1999.

Osherson, Samuel. *Wrestling with Love: How Men Struggle with Intimacy with Women, Children, Parents, and Each Other.* New York: Random House, 1992.

———. *Finding Our Fathers: How a Man's Life Is Shaped by His Relationship with His Father.* New York: McGraw-Hill, 1986.

Parke, Ross D., and Armin Brott. *Throwaway Dads: The Myths and Barriers that Keep Men from Being the Fathers They Want To Be.* Boston: Houghton Mifflin, 1999.

Peurifoy, Reneau Z. *Overcoming Anxiety: From Short-Term Fixes to Long-Term Recovery.* New York: Henry Holt, 1997.

Pollack, William. *Real Boys.* New York: Henry Holt, 1995.

Poulter, Stephan B. *Father Your Son: How To Become the Father You Have Always Wanted to Be.* New York: McGraw-Hill, 2004.

Poulter, Stephan B., and Barbara Zax. *Mending the Broken Bough: Restoring the Promise of the Mother-Daughter Relationship.* New York: Berkley Publishers, 1998.

Pruett, Kyle D. *Fatherneed: Why Father Care Is as Essential as Mother Care for Your Child.* New York: Free Press, 2000.

Real, T. *I Don't Want To Talk about It: Overcoming the Secret Legacy of Male Depression.* New York: Scribner, 1997.

Ricci, Isolina. *Mom's House, Dad's House: A Complete Guide for Parents Who Are Separated, Divorced, or Remarried.* New York: Fireside, 1997.

Rolfe, Randy. *The 7 Secrets of Successful Parents.* Chicago: Contemporary Books, 1997.

Shaffer, Susan M., and Linda P. Gordon. *Why Girls Talk—And What They're Really Saying: A Parent's Survival Guide to Connecting with Your Teen.* New York: McGraw-Hill, 2005.

Shapiro, Jerold L. *The Measure of a Man: Becoming the Father You Wish Your Father Had Been.* New York: Berkley Publishing Group, 1995.

Sheehan, David V. *The Anxiety Disease.* New York: Scribner, 1983.

Simon, Sidney B., and Suzanne Simon. *Forgiveness: How to Make Peace with Your Past and Get on with Your Life.* New York: Warner Books, 1990.

Slipp, Samuel. *Object Relations: A Dynamic Bridge between Individual and Family Treatment.* New York: Jason Aronson, 1991.

Smedes, Lewis B. *Forgive & Forget: Healing the Hurts We Don't Deserve.* San Francisco: Harper & Row, 1984.

Theobald, Theo, and Cary Cooper. *Shut Up and Listen!: The Truth about How to Communicate at Work.* Sterling, VA; Kogan Page, 2004.

Tracy, Brian. *Maximum Achievement: The Proven System of Strategies and Skills That Will Unlock Your Hidden Powers to Succeed.* New York: Simon & Schuster, 1995.

Winston, Stephanie. *Organized for Success: Top Executives and CEOs Reveal the Organizing Principles That Helped Them Reach the Top.* New York: Crown Business, 2004.

Zieghan, Suzen J. *The Stepparent's Survival Guide. A Workbook for Creating a Happy Blended Family.* Oakland, CA: New Harbinger Publications, 2002.

Zukav, Gary. *Seat of the Soul.* New York: Simon & Schuster, 1990.

# INDEX